LEMNOS

Troy

LESBOS

GOLDEN
DRINKING CUP

ANATOLIA
(ASIA MINOR)

Marathon

Athens

ATTICA

ANDROS

• Ephesus

KEA

CYCLADES

SAMOS

IKARIA

SYROS

DELOS

AEGEAN SEA

PAROS    NAXOS

MELOS

IOS

THERA

Akrotiri

RHODES

EARTH
GODDESS

SEA OF CRETE

KARPATHOS

ydonia

• Knossos    Gournia

CRETE         • Mallia

Myrtos    Basilike

Phaistos                Zakros

*Cover:* In a royal shaft grave at Mycenae, archaeologist Heinrich Schliemann unearthed this mask, hammered from a heavy sheet of gold. Impressed by its strong, Greek features, he erroneously believed that it had been made for Agamemnon, leader of the siege of Troy. Here the majestic visage, created about 1600 BC, appears against a view of the Lion Gate, the main portal to Mycenae's citadel. About 10 feet square and almost a yard thick, the gate was named for reliefs of two lions, now headless, carved on a limestone slab above the lintel.

*End paper:* Painted by artist Paul Breeden on paper textured to resemble a fresco surface, the map highlights Aegean cities and sites in the Bronze Age. Mycenae is marked by its Lion Gate, Knossos by an earth-goddess statue, Troy by a golden drinking cup, and Thera by swallows from a fresco. A gold charm from Crete, formed of two honeybees, points north. The inset locates the Aegean realms in the wider context of the Mediterranean.

# WONDROUS REALMS OF THE AEGEAN

Time-Life Books is a division of Time Life Inc., a wholly owned subsidiary of **THE TIME INC. BOOK COMPANY**

**TIME-LIFE BOOKS**

PRESIDENT: Mary N. Davis

MANAGING EDITOR: Thomas H. Flaherty
*Director of Editorial Resources:* Elise D. Ritter-Clough
*Executive Art Director:* Ellen Robling
*Director of Photography and Research:* John Conrad Weiser
*Editorial Board:* Dale M. Brown, Janet Cave, Roberta Conlan, Laura Foreman, Jim Hicks, Blaine Marshall, Rita Thievon Mullin, Henry Woodhead
*Assistant Director of Editorial Resources/Training Manager:* Norma E. Shaw

PUBLISHER: Robert H. Smith

*Associate Publisher:* Sandra Lafe Smith
*Editorial Director:* Russell B. Adams, Jr.
*Marketing Director:* Anne C. Everhart
*Director of Production Services:* Robert N. Carr
*Production Manager:* Prudence G. Harris
*Supervisor of Quality Control:* James King

Editorial Operations
*Production:* Celia Beattie
*Library:* Louise D. Forstall
*Computer Composition:* Deborah G. Tait (Manager), Monika D. Thayer, Janet Barnes Syring, Lillian Daniels
*Interactive Media Specialist:* Patti H. Cass

**Library of Congress
Cataloging in Publication Data**
Wondrous realms of the Aegean / by the editors of Time-Life Books.
p. cm.—(Lost civilizations)
Includes bibliographical references and index.
ISBN 0-8094-9875-8 (trade)
ISBN 0-8094-9876-6 (lib. bdg.)
1. Aegean Sea Region—Antiquities. 2. Civilization, Aegean. 3. Bronze Age—Aegean Sea Region. 4. Excavations (Archaeology)—Aegean Sea Region. I. Time-Life Books. II. Series.
DF220.W66   1993
939.1—dc20
92-29449

**LOST CIVILIZATIONS**

SERIES EDITOR: Dale M. Brown
*Series Administrator:* Philip Brandt George

Editorial staff for: *Wondrous Realms of the Aegean*
*Art Director:* Susan K. White
*Picture Editor:* Kristin Baker Hanneman
*Text Editors:* Charlotte Anker (principal), James M. Lynch
*Writers:* Darcie Conner Johnston, Denise Dersin
*Associate Editors/Research:* Constance Contreras, Jacqueline L. Shaffer
*Assistant Editor/Research:* Katherine L. Griffin
*Assistant Art Director:* Bill McKenney
*Senior Copy Coordinator:* Anne Farr
*Picture Coordinator:* David A. Herod
*Editorial Assistant:* Patricia D. Whiteford

*Special Contributors:* Beryl Lieff Benderly, Arlene Borden, Douglas Botting, Windsor Chorlton, George Constable, Ellen Galford, Susan Morse, Lydia Preston-Hicks, Michelle D. Vaughen (text); Helga Kohl, Jocelyn G. Lindsay, Aziza Meer, Gail Prensky, Evelyn Prettyman, Eugenia S. Scharf (research); Roy Nanovic (index)

*Correspondents:* Elisabeth Kraemer-Singh (Bonn), Christine Hinze (London), Christina Lieberman (New York), Maria Vincenza Aloisi (Paris), Ann Natanson (Rome). Valuable assistance was also provided by: Maria Chadou, Daphne Gondicas, Mirka Gondicas, Aristotle Sarricostas (Athens); Nihal Tamraz (Cairo); Judy Aspinall (London); Elizabeth Brown, Katheryn White (New York); Ann Wise (Rome).

*The Consultants:*
James C. Wright, professor of classical and prehistoric archaeology at Bryn Mawr College, has been excavating in Greece since 1973. For more than a decade, he has directed the Nemea Valley Archaeological Project, a multidisciplinary study of the valley between ancient Mycenae and Corinth.

Jeremy B. Rutter, professor of classics at Dartmouth College and an expert in Bronze Age chronology, spent more than 15 years excavating at various sites in southern Greece. Recently he has worked as chief ceramics analyst for a dig at the Minoan harbor town of Kommos, on Crete.

George F. Bass founded the Institute of Nautical Archaeology at Texas A&M University, where he is Abell Professor of Nautical Archaeology. He recently directed the excavation of the world's oldest shipwreck *(pages 147-157)*, dating to the 14th century BC.

Diana Keeran Withee, a scholar in art history and archaeology, is program coordinator of the Teacher and School Programs for the National Gallery of Art in Washington, D.C. She has written on issues relating to the preservation of Theran frescoes.

*For information on and a full description of any of the Time-Life Books series listed above, please call 1-800-621-7026 or write:*
Reader Information
Time-Life Customer Service
P.O. Box C-32068
Richmond, Virginia 23261-2068

This volume is one in a series that explores the worlds of the past, using the finds of archaeologists and other scientists to bring ancient peoples and their cultures vividly to life.

# WONDROUS REALMS OF THE AEGEAN

By the Editors of Time-Life Books

**TIME-LIFE BOOKS, ALEXANDRIA, VIRGINIA**

# CONTENTS

*A finger of the Aegean Sea pokes into a cove on the island of Melos, in the Cyclades, brushing the sun-drenched ruins of Phylokapi (foreground). Three successive Bronze Age cities have been found in layers here, and below them, remnants of the Stone Age. The last settlement flourished in the middle of the second millennium BC. Melos was a prime source of obsidian, the glass-like volcanic stone used for making sharp-edged blades and tools.*

# IN SEARCH OF LEGENDARY KINGDOMS

**T**he hill is sandy, rock-strewn, entirely unprepossessing in appearance. Yet it happens to be one of the most exciting archaeological sites in the world, a 160-foot-high mound composed of the ruins of ancient cities layered one on top of the other. Beneath its rough contours lie no fewer than 10 Troys, spanning 3,500 years of history from the Early Bronze Age to Roman times. In 1988, scores of scientists from Germany, Austria, Denmark, Britain, Mexico, the United States, and Turkey flocked to this spot in northwestern Turkey, some three miles south of the Dardanelles, the strait that separates Europe from Asia, to begin their digging. The task was enormous, and they would have to return year after year for additional summers of excavation.

Hissarlik, as the hill is called, lies at the head of the Aegean Sea, birthplace of the first European civilizations. To the west a chain of small jewel-like isles, resplendent in their vast turquoise settings, strings out toward mainland Greece, where talons of land, edged with natural harbors, stretch into the sun-streaked waters. From the tip of Attica, the southeastern region of Greece, a wreath of islands, the Cyclades, circles the southern Aegean. They lead farther south toward the elongated, mountain-spined isle of Crete and the wider Mediterranean beyond.

While most of mainland Europe still lived in huts, the peoples

*Gleaming as on the day it was made nearly 3,600 years ago, this hammered gold rhyton, or drinking vessel, in the shape of a lion's head emerged from a grave at Mycenae, home to some of the ancient world's most famous warriors.*

9

of these islands, like those of Troy, were flourishing. They roamed far and wide in their ships, built great palaces, developed writing, enjoyed an unusually high standard of living, and created wall paintings that rivaled those of Egypt, concurrently experiencing its golden age. Yet by the time of Jesus, these early inhabitants of the Aegean were lost to memory. Then, at Hissarlik, more than a century ago, an entrepreneur-turned-archaeologist lifted the veil of oblivion.

Today, Hissarlik is carved into a confusion of trenches and pits that slice down through time. Among its levels of settlement lie the ruins of the fortress-city that was the setting for one of the greatest of all works of literature, Homer's *Iliad,* composed some 2,700 years ago. This verse epic is an incomparably powerful tale, propelled by emotions that range from implacable rage to every sort of love—sexual passion, the bonds of parent and child, the warrior's love of glory in combat. The story recounts the climactic weeks of a 10-year war of revenge: King Agamemnon and a great force from what is today the Greek mainland, and from Crete, seek to punish Troy because one of its princes, hot-blooded Paris, has seduced and made off with the outstanding beauty of the day—Helen, queen of Sparta and wife of Agamemnon's brother, Menelaus.

At the center of the story is the inevitable confrontation of two mighty warriors: the near-invincible Achilles, in league with Agamemnon, and Hector the Trojan. Destiny, effected by the ever-manipulative gods, brings them together for the last time in the swirling dust on the Trojan plain. Hector is overmatched but valiant to the end: "So Hector swooped now, swinging his whetted sword and Achilles charged too, bursting with rage, barbaric, guarding his chest with the well-wrought blazoned shield." Against the rage and ferocity of Achilles, Hector has no chance; nor does any other Trojan warrior. But Troy continues to resist successfully until the forces of Agamemnon pretend to retreat and then insinuate men into the fortress by hiding them within a wooden horse—a ploy related in Homer's other great work, the *Odyssey*.

With such a tale attached to this place—of clashing spears and shields, of valor, perfidy, and passion—it is little wonder scholars are drawn to Hissarlik. Their interest, however, is of comparatively recent vintage. The mound came to light in the latter part of the 19th century because a self-taught German excavator named Heinrich

10

*During the time of Homeric Troy, merchant ships anchored at nearby Besike Bay, which was bigger then than now. While awaiting favorable sailing conditions, some mariners inevitably sickened and died. Their remains were buried in a headland cemetery discovered in 1984.*

Schliemann—brilliant, driven, obsessed both with making money and with recovering the past—was convinced that, in some form or other, the *Iliad* had actually happened, presumably around 1250 BC, the date assigned by ancient Greek tradition.

Schliemann's fascination with Homer ultimately led him to uncover another legendary people, the Mycenaeans, who lived on the Peloponnesus, where eventually a Greek civilization would arise. Coalescing as a culture as early as 1600 BC and fading into oblivion around 1050 BC, the Mycenaeans were individualists with strong appetites, especially for the excitements of war and the hunt. They constructed massive, great-halled fortresses, took to the sea in ever-larger numbers of ships, and projected their power at spearpoint throughout the Aegean.

But the Mycenaeans themselves proved to be heirs to an earlier, even more sophisticated culture—that of the Minoans of Crete. On the heels of Schliemann's finds, another wealthy archaeologist, Sir Arthur Evans of Britain, discovered this older Aegean people, finding them to be less martial, more communal, marvelously gifted in crafts, art, and architecture. And soon other archaeologists pushed the story of Aegean civilization even further back in time, to the fourth millennium BC, an era that ushered in the Bronze Age. During that period precocious societies developed on virtually all the islands of the Aegean, especially the central ring of them known as the Cyclades, a necklace strung between the Peloponnesus and southwestern Turkey. Troy was thus merely the starting point for a great modern epic of archaeological discovery, with legions of scholars pursuing studies of the Mycenaeans, the Minoans, and the Cycladic societies at sites around Homer's wine-dark sea.

The international team excavating Hissarlik in the summer of 1988 was led by the German prehistorian Manfred Korfmann, who put a new spin on the greatest war story ever told. It seemed apparent to Korfmann, on the basis of a discovery he had made in the early 1980s, that sea trade, not the beautiful and wayward Helen, was the probable cause of the Trojan War. Korfmann had uncovered, about five miles southwest of Hissarlik, a mariners' cemetery dating to the 13th century BC, the time of Homeric Troy. Unlike most ancient cemeteries, this one had accommodated strikingly diverse funeral practices: Some of the dead had been cremated; others had been buried, but in various types of graves. Since no settlement could be found, Korfmann assumed that these people had lived here temporarily, in makeshift shelters. He reasoned that the cemetery was associated with transient trading communities made up of merchants from different lands as well as the crews needed to navigate the ships that held their merchandise.

Trading in cargoes of precious metal, pottery, wine, oil, and other goods, the merchants were attempting to make it through the Dardanelles out into the open sea, one of the more difficult passages of Aegean traffic. Into that narrow strait drains the Black Sea, fed by the great rivers of eastern Europe and the Eurasian Steppes—the Danube, Don, Dnieper, Bug, and Dniester. The rush of waters into the strait produces a contrary current that averages three miles per hour and sometimes reaches five. With a wind at her back, an ancient sailing ship could conquer the current, but even in summer the winds were mostly adverse, blowing from the north. And in the stormy winter months, when storms raged, there was no venturing forth into the wind-whipped sea at all. (Seafarers would not learn how to sail against the wind until the early Christian era.)

Often a cargo-laden ship had to put in at a harbor close to the entrance of the strait and wait for days, weeks, or even months until conditions permitted passage. This situation was very much to Troy's advantage, since it had the nearest harbor, Besike Bay, a coastal indentation in the lee of a headland that blocks the winds rushing down the strait. The sheltered bay was a perfect place for an ancient mariner to pass the time until the weather took a turn for the better. And it was at the northern end of Besike Bay that Korfmann had uncovered the mariners' cemetery.

Besike Bay, Korfmann concluded, was a scene of lively commerce, largely because ships were forced to stop and linger there. The fortress of Troy nearby probably would have demanded a share of the profits from this traffic, perhaps by de-

A sandstone frieze on a tomb in Asia Minor illustrates scenes from Homer's epics, the Iliad and the Odyssey. One part of the fourth-century BC bas-relief (above, top) may depict the Trojan Hector and the Greek Achilles in hand-to-hand combat. The section below shows the Trojans defending their battlements by hurling stones at the invading Greeks.

A Roman copy of a Greek sculpture of Homer portrays the poet as an aging man, with lifeless eyes. So little is known of Homer that his supposed blindness may be a myth. It is not even certain he composed the poems on which his fame rests.

manding fees for allowing boats to be anchored in the harbor or beached on the shore, and for food or other services. Merchants, held hostage by the winds, had little choice except to pay.

By virtue of its muscle and location, Troy grew rich. But at the same time it also became a target, Korfmann reasons. Traders from mainland Greece and elsewhere who resented the tolls the inhabitants imposed, or who simply coveted Troy's gold, may well have returned, well armed and in force, to besiege the city, burning and looting it—and perhaps more than once. By Homer's day, Korfmann speculates, the passing centuries had blurred those events and elevated them from slashing raids, motivated by resentment or avarice, to the 10-year campaign celebrated by Homer, waged by huge armies for honor and martial glory.

Homer's identity is wrapped in mystery, but the poet probably composed the *Iliad* and the *Odyssey* sometime around 750-700 BC, when early Greece was struggling out of its so-called Dark Ages following the collapse of Mycenaean culture about 1050 BC. This bleak period was characterized by simple agricultural villages and illiteracy. Until early in the first millennium BC, the whole corpus of tradition had been transmitted orally, with successive generations of taletellers presumably memorizing the words of their elders. Homer himself was an oral poet, a master of inherited lore. Many other folk tales—transmitted from generation to generation by storytellers—also told of the deeds of gods, heroes, and ordinary mortals in the remote past.

To the Greeks of the classical era (700-200 BC), Homer's epics were genuine historical accounts of their ancestors, descriptions of real people and events. This was also the time of the playwrights Aeschylus, Sophocles, and Euripides. These intellectual titans recast the ancient stories into powerful dramas that continue to move audiences the world over.

Inevitably, Troy was raised to the status of a Greek shrine. In 334 BC, the Macedonian conqueror Alexander the Great stopped at Troy after crossing into Asia on his way to fight the king of Persia. He honored the spot by sacrificing to the gods, rubbing his body with oil, and running naked—the customary procedure at funeral games for Greek notables—around the supposed tomb of Achilles, whose spirit, he felt, lived on in himself. Throughout his campaigns, Alexander carried with him a tattered copy of the *Iliad* written on a papyrus scroll, and allegedly slept with it beneath his head.

# MYTH OR REALITY? GETTING TO THE BOTTOM OF THE TROJAN HORSE STORY

The world's most famous piece of military equipment, the Trojan Horse, may—or may not—have existed. But if it did, in all likelihood the horse looked quite different from the traditional descriptions and representations of it.

Mentioned in passing by Homer in the *Iliad,* it was featured in Virgil's first-century AD epic poem, the *Aeneid,* which tells how the hero Aeneas escaped from besieged Troy to found the Roman state. As time went on, the Trojan Horse became more and more a creature of fantasy. By the fifth century AD, the Greek poet Tryphiodorus described it as white, with a purple-and-gold mane, eyes of green beryl and red amethyst, and teeth of ivory. Artists further embellished its image.

Ironically, it may be art that offers a clue to what the horse may really have been. In the eighth-century BC relief seen below, warring Assyrians make use of a battering ram to get at their enemies. This siege machine was a wheeled wooden contraption operated from within by a handful of men. Whether a similar but much earlier device was employed to batter down Troy's gate and admit the Greeks to the walled city can of course never be established as a certainty, but it remains a possibility.

Whatever the reality behind the oft-repeated legend, the visitor to Troy today is greeted by a fake, three-story-tall Trojan Horse *(background),* assembled from lumber by local Turks as a tourist attraction.

*Above, in an Assyrian relief, a wooden siege machine of a type that may have been the inspiration for the Trojan Horse story rams a fortress in the Near Eastern city of Upa. Right, an eighth-century BC amphora discovered on the island of Mykonos bears the earliest known representation of the mythical Trojan Horse.*

The unsuspecting people of Troy struggle to pull the horse filled with Greeks into their city in an 18th-century painting by Giovanni Domenico Tiepolo. The Venetian artist gave the horse and scene the rococo flourishes common in his era.

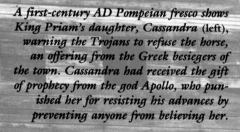

A first-century AD Pompeian fresco shows King Priam's daughter, Cassandra (left), warning the Trojans to refuse the horse, an offering from the Greek besiegers of the town. Cassandra had received the gift of prophecy from the god Apollo, who punished her for resisting his advances by preventing anyone from believing her.

By the early sixth century AD, habitation at Troy had winked out altogether. Throughout succeeding centuries, the name of Troy—Ilium to the last occupiers, the Romans—was bandied about the Aegean region, but its exact whereabouts had faded from Western memory. When, in the 15th century, a great Renaissance literary revival was wrought by the invention of movable type, and the first printed edition of Homer was published in Florence in 1488, Agamemnon, Achilles, Hector, and Helen once again became fixed in the educated mind. But the *Iliad* and the *Odyssey* were no longer read as testimony to real events. Scholars were unable to trace Greek history further back than the eighth century BC, when the first Olympic Games were staged. Prior centuries were almost impenetrably dim; the meager surviving evidence of that era suggested that the Aegean realm had been backward, mired in poverty and ignorance, fractured by endless warfare. The Homeric vision of palaces, treasure, and heroic ideals was a mirage, scholars agreed. It would take a singularly imaginative man to overthrow this view.

Heinrich Schliemann, the discoverer of Troy, was not only imaginative but showed himself to be possessed of a swift intelligence, a prodigious memory, and boundless energy. Some said he was also selfish, boastful, and mendacious. Born in a small German village in 1822, one of six children of a pastor, Schliemann knew little happiness as a child. His father drank heavily, conducted an open affair with a housemaid, and treated his wife with contempt. Decades later, the son would paint a wistful and romantic picture of these years in his autobiographical writings, telling of a girl he had loved, boyhood adventures among the local ruins, and an early fascination with the legend of Troy. He claimed that at the age of seven, he became convinced of the historical veracity of the Trojan War and vowed he would someday find and excavate the Homeric citadel. Recently some scholars have come to believe that he displayed no interest in Troy until

surprisingly late in life. They base this conclusion on the fact that in his peripatetic early years, he chose to tour many countries but did not visit Greece until he was in his forties. And Schliemann took liberties with the truth throughout his life. Still, he was an avid reader in his boyhood, and it seems plausible that, having devoured Homer, he gave full rein to his imagination and came up with extravagant fantasies.

In his 14th year, new miseries closed in on Schliemann. The family fell into penury after his father was suspended from the ministry for philandering and possible embezzlement. Heinrich, a promising student, was withdrawn from school and sent to work as a servant in a grocery shop in another village. There he spent almost five years, performing menial duties. Finally, desperately unhappy, he left the shop for the port of Hamburg, determined to go to America. When he was unable to borrow the money for his passage, he signed on as a ship's boy aboard a vessel bound for South America. The voyage was brief and catastrophic. The ship was overtaken by a great storm in the North Sea and sank off the coast of Holland. Schliemann survived by clinging to a cask for hours until he was picked up by a lifeboat.

After facing a watery death, he lost, temporarily, his desire to cross the Atlantic. Instead, he joined a firm of merchants in Amsterdam, as a clerk. His employers soon realized that this was no ordinary lad. He was quick with figures, observing and remembering the smallest details of the business. Above all, he had drive—a fierce, single-minded, all-consuming desire to succeed.

Success in trade meant learning other languages, and Schliemann, who spent nothing on pleasure or comfort, had few friends, and went nowhere, committed every spare minute to the task, staying awake far into the night by drinking quantities of sugared tea. Memorizing long lists of words, he taught himself English in six months and French after another half year. Still, he found the process too slow, so he devised a system of reading and writing exercises that he said gave him mastery of any language in just six weeks. Within two

*Outside the cabin in which the archaeologist and his Greek wife, Sophia, lived while excavating Troy, Schliemann, seated, poses with his assistant Wilhelm Dörpfeld, seen immediately behind him, and visitors. Nearby, Schliemann had unearthed several giant storage jars (engraving), one of which was moved to the site of the living quarters and served a workman as a nighttime shelter.*

*An 1880 photo shows Sophia, with the couple's children, Andromache and Agamemnon. At their first meeting, Sophia won Heinrich's heart by reciting from the Iliad. So much a Grecophile was Schliemann that he claimed to have regularly massaged Agamemnon's nose in an attempt to give him a classic Greek profile.*

years or so of his first job in Amsterdam, he was corresponding with other merchants in English, French, Dutch, Spanish, Italian, and Portuguese. Eventually he would be fluent in a dozen tongues.

The most valuable language for his burgeoning career was Russian, which he mastered in 1844. Two years later, he was sent to St. Petersburg to manage the firm's affairs there. He was hardly a commanding figure—only 24 years old, short, homely, with a shrill voice and a high-strung manner. But such were his talents that he soon amassed a fortune trading in raw materials. Part of his genius lay in his insatiable thirst for information, some of which came from local contacts or from the ceaseless stream of letters he wrote standing at his upright desk. His energy was matched by an ability to take huge risks, and the tensions produced by his business life were vented in volcanic rages and wild boasting to anyone who would listen.

In 1850, he received word that his younger brother Ludwig had died of typhus in California, where he had reportedly gotten rich on the gold recently discovered in streambeds. Schliemann decided to claim the money. On the trip, he kept a detailed diary—a lifelong habit of self-reporting that was supplemented by the tens of thousands of letters he wrote and the 18 journals and 12 books he would eventually publish about his life and work. Perhaps he already sensed that biographers would be interested in his career; in any event, he began to embellish it. Among the fabrications in his diary was a tale of attending a large reception in Washington and having a long conversation with President Millard Fillmore and his wife; the event apparently never took place.

Brother Ludwig's fortune proved as illusory as the president's fete. In Sacramento, Schliemann began buying and selling gold dust, and within nine months he had made $400,000, a stupendous sum at the time. He returned to Russia, feeling secure enough to settle down and raise a family. His choice of a mate was the daughter of a Russian merchant—a handsome, somewhat haughty woman, who bore him three children. But Schliemann continued working at a rate that left little time for family life. He gained control of the market in indigo, a dyestuff. He invested in real estate. With the outbreak of the Crimean War in 1854, he became the most adroit of profiteers, dealing in the saltpeter and sulfur used to make gunpowder and the lead needed for bullets. But no matter how high his riches piled, he remained dissatisfied, unhappy in his marriage, and gnawed by a need to prove his worth.

He left Russia, moving first to Dresden, then to Paris in 1866, where he studied languages at the Sorbonne and invested in properties. His wife stayed in St. Petersburg, hardly bothering to reply to his letters. In the early summer of 1868, he visited the Greek island of Ithaca, the Peloponnesus, and the portion of Asia Minor said to have been the scene of the Trojan War. The tour changed his life.

Among Schliemann's many interests was the literature of ancient Greece. Now the Aegean and its environs, vibrant with literary and historical associations, awoke in him a deep attraction to Greek traditions and a sense that, with his resources and abilities, he could be a true investigator rather than a mere visitor. Indeed, the secret to success seemed quite clear to him: One simply had to have faith in the essential accuracy of Homer.

This premise was first put to the test on Ithaca, the island home of the legendary hero Odysseus, who had fought in the Trojan War and then, as recounted in the *Odyssey,* spent 10 years wending his way back to his wife, Penelope. When Schliemann arrived in Ithaca, he wrote, "Every hill, every stone, every stream, every olive grove reminded me of Homer, and so I found myself with a single leap hurled across a hundred generations into the glittering age of Greek knighthood." Determined to make contact with that age, Schliemann hired four laborers and went to Mount Aëtos, where, according to legend, Odysseus' palace once stood. The workmen, digging at the corner of a stone wall, came upon two urns containing ashes. Thrilled, Schliemann wrote in his diary, "It is quite possible that they contain the ashes of Odysseus and Penelope, or their descendants."

Such flights of fancy marked Schliemann's entire archaeological career. Over and over again in the years ahead, he would jump to conclusions that were, at best, unwarranted and that led many professional archaeologists to brand him a headline seeker. Yet Schliemann's renegade speculations would yield genuine miracles of discovery.

His first great find occurred at Troy. In 1868, he set out to reconnoiter the reputed locale of the Trojan War and—with an eye

*A marble relief sculpture found by Schliemann at Hissarlik—and once displayed in his Athens garden—depicts the sun god Phoebus Apollo. The relief, dating from the fourth to the middle of the second century BC, shows Apollo with his four horses at the start of a daily journey to bring light to the world.*

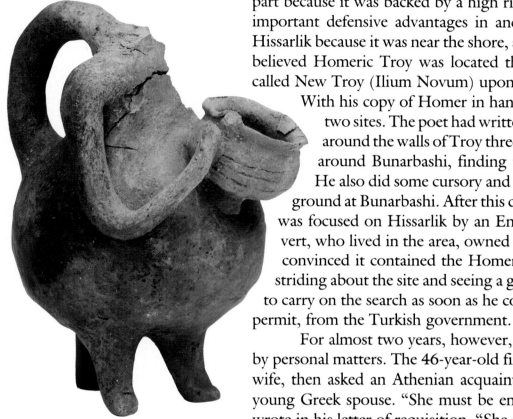

*A modeled clay pitcher from one of the early settlements of Troy (ca. 2600-1800 BC) is unusual because of its unique treatment of the human form. The filling hole for the vessel was in the head, now missing, while the small bowl on the figure's belly served as the spout.*

to future digs—pick the likeliest spot for the Homeric citadel. There were two candidates. One was the site of a village called Bunarbashi, about five miles inland from the Aegean; the other was the hill of Hissarlik, almost three miles from the sea. Of the scholars willing to contemplate the possible reality of Troy, most favored Bunarbashi, in part because it was backed by a high ridge that would have offered important defensive advantages in ancient times. Some preferred Hissarlik because it was near the shore, and because the Romans had believed Homeric Troy was located there; they had built a town called New Troy (Ilium Novum) upon the mound.

With his copy of Homer in hand, Schliemann examined the two sites. The poet had written of Achilles chasing Hector around the walls of Troy three times, and so he tried to run around Bunarbashi, finding the hill impossible to circle. He also did some cursory and unproductive probing of the ground at Bunarbashi. After this disappointment, his attention was focused on Hissarlik by an Englishman named Frank Calvert, who lived in the area, owned part of this mound, and was convinced it contained the Homeric city. His German visitor, striding about the site and seeing a good fit with the *Iliad,* vowed to carry on the search as soon as he could get a *firman,* or digging permit, from the Turkish government.

For almost two years, however, Schliemann was sidetracked by personal matters. The 46-year-old financier divorced his Russian wife, then asked an Athenian acquaintance to find him a suitable young Greek spouse. "She must be enthusiatic about Homer," he wrote in his letter of requisition. "She should be of the Greek type, with black hair and, if possible, beautiful. But the main requirement is a good and loving heart." He promptly married one of the suggested candidates, 17-year-old Sophia Engastromenos, who—to the perpetual amazement of her husband—did turn out to be a warm-hearted woman who would be an active partner in his archaeological endeavors. With Sophia he fathered two children, a daughter whom Schliemann christened Andromache, after Hector's wife, and a son upon whom he bestowed the name of the leader of the confederation that defeated Troy—Agamemnon.

In 1870, though not yet granted a firman, Schliemann returned to Hissarlik for 13 days of digging. His illegal excavations were halted by the Turks who owned the land he was excavating, for he had spurned Calvert's property, choosing instead the part of the

# THE UNSOLVED CASE OF THE MISSING GOLD OF TROY

To the outrage of the Turkish government, Heinrich Schliemann bequeathed to Germany the fabulous cache of gold, the so-called Treasure of Priam, that he had unearthed at Troy and proudly put on display in his Athens home. For 55 years following his death the array of vessels, weapons, and jewelry remained a prize possession of Berlin's State Museum for Pre- and Early History.

During World War II the gold rested in a concrete bunker for safekeeping, but disappeared toward the end of hostilities when Soviet troops seized the sector of the city where the museum was located. The Soviet gov-ernment denied having taken the cache. Scholars and admirers despaired, presuming the treasure lost forever—destroyed during heavy fighting or massive air assaults, or melted for quick sale by looting Soviet soldiers.

But hope that the trove still exists was awakened in 1990 when a Russian archaeologist reported that it had been seen in Moscow in the 1960s. This would seem to be corroborated by the discovery of shipping vouchers from Berlin and itemized receipts from Moscow for a 1945 consignment that included the treasure. And there the mystery stands: The hoard's present location remains unknown.

*Sophia Schliemann* (above, left), *the archaeologist's Greek wife, models gold jewelry from the diggings at Troy: four intricately wrought earrings—two dangling from her neckline—an elaborate diadem, and a necklace.*

*Reproduced by Yemenite jewelers from photographs of the missing original, the diadem from the Treasure of Priam* (above) *is made up of 106 chains consisting of 12,271 links and 4,066 tiny gold sheets of various shapes.*

Schliemann's photo of his find shows the treasure at his Athens home. Gold jewelry is displayed above the bookcase. Silver and electrum cups, copper weapons, and various vessels, including a large one-handled silver mug in which the smaller ornaments turned up, line other shelves. The copper shield and the cauldron at the bottom display ancient fire damage.

The double-lipped drinking cup below, perhaps designed to be shared by host and guest, was re-created for an exhibit in 1990 in Berlin and Athens. The original, of 23-carat gold, weighed 1.2 pounds.

mound facing the sea. In that brief burst of work, he managed to uncover some impressive stone walls, which he described as "six feet thick and of most wonderful construction," part of a building 60 feet long and 40 feet wide. Thrilled, Schliemann harbored not the slightest doubt that he had proven the reality of Homer.

Still, it took a year of cajoling and threatening Turkish officials before Schliemann was finally granted a firman. He then hired a force of 120 workmen and, from October to November, cut a deep trench into the hill. To his amazement, he found a multitude of Troys—walls built upon walls, one city upon another, a clutter of stonework, pottery, and artifact fragments. Certain that Homeric Troy was the oldest city on the site, he rushed to the bottom of the mound, discarding or demolishing what got in his way. His ruthless digging would earn him such epithets as "graverobber" or "the second destroyer of Troy" from some of the scholars of his day.

Returning in the spring of 1872, he reaffirmed his "unshakable faith in Homer." Yet his greatest find of the season was Hellenistic. He discovered a large marble relief of Apollo riding the four horses of the sun, dated from the fourth to the mid-second century BC. In the art world the sculpture was declared a masterpiece, and he

was especially delighted by "the four horses which, snorting and looking wildly forward, career through the atmosphere of the universe with infinite power." While professing little interest in finds not from the Homeric period, nonetheless Schliemann smuggled the Apollo out of the country and kept it in his garden at Athens.

As he poked about the lower strata the following year, he found rudimentary pottery and tools made of stone. His spirits began to wilt at such meager pickings, but he pressed on with his huge work force. And suddenly the depths of the mound began to disgorge the sort of evidence he sought. In April, he hit upon a paved street and some immense earthenware storage jars, suggestive of a well-developed economy. Find followed find. In May, he unearthed what he had been seeking—a large building that he designated "the ruins of the palace of the last king of Troy, who is called Priam by Homer and all classical tradition." In front lay remnants of two great stone structures. These, he decided, had been the Scaean Gate—scene of one of the most moving moments in the *Iliad,* when Hector says good-bye to his wife, Andromache, before going forth to battle.

At the end of May came a find whose extraordinary nature was beyond debate. In a wall of the building he took to be Priam's palace,

*A contemporary panoramic view of the Schliemanns' excavation of Mycenae on the Greek mainland* (below) *includes Sophia* (foreground) *and Heinrich* (right center in fedora), *with workers lined up in the background, at the site of Grave Circle A. In the photograph at left, Schliemann leans on one of the headless lions for which the citadel's impressive gate is named. His assistant Dörpfeld sits in the opening in the wall at upper left while Sophia stays below with visitors. The 10-foot-high limestone relief from the 13th century BC is the oldest Greek monumental sculpture known.*

Schliemann spotted a gleam of gold. According to his later account of the episode, he sent the workmen away on a ruse. Then he began to dig with his pocketknife, describing the task later as "the most fearful risk to my life, for the great fortification wall, beneath which I had to dig, threatened every moment to fall down upon me." At last he unearthed a trove of golden objects. He would explain that the treasure must have been packed, for a quick departure, in a "wooden trunk like those mentioned in the *Iliad* as having been in Priam's palace." He and his wife slipped away, carrying the gold of Troy in Sophia's embroidered scarlet shawl.

This bit of drama, believed for nearly a century, was recently shown to have been invented. Among the inaccuracies was the site of discovery: In a magazine interview in 1878, Nikolaos Yannakis, one of Schliemann's most trusted workmen, stated that this was not the palace wall but a tomb outside the building. Whatever the reality, however, Hissarlik had yielded a true treasure—a dazzling heap of gold that totaled nearly 10,000 articles. By creating a smuggling network of Sophia's relatives, Schliemann spirited the trove out of the country and beyond Turkish reach, then informed the world of his triumph. He had found, he said, the treasure of King Priam.

He had not. Schliemann was off by about 1,000 years. In his frenetic drive to reach the bottom of the mound, he had slashed through seven layers without recognizing them, finding the gold at the eighth level. (There was also a ninth stratum that lay beneath the one that held the treasure, and the digs that began in 1988 would uncover still earlier remains.) Each of these strata was a city built on the town beneath. The bottom stratum, later known as Troy I, dated as far back as 3000 BC, almost two millennia before Homer's citadel was beset by Agamemnon's armies. The hoard of gold had come from the next layer, which would subsequently be called Troy II and attributed to a period before 2000 BC. Like Homer's Troy, which had been ravaged by fire, the buildings of this era had been burned as well. In the

*The gold diadem at right, a royal crown or headband, was among the treasures relinquished by the Circle A shaft graves in Mycenae. Gold objects that had been specially made as funerary offerings were often placed on a sarcophagus or shroud as well as directly on the dead.*

*Gold plates decorated with naturalistic themes adorn a hexagonal wooden pyxis, or cosmetic box, from Shaft Grave V at Mycenae. The design of the 16th-century BC reliefs represents a fusion of diverse Aegean motifs in a style that is distinctly and vigorously Mycenaean.*

*Under a blazing sun and a crescent moon, a nature goddess receives offerings of flowers from devotees in a ceremony portrayed on a gold signet ring found at Mycenae. The scene, measuring only an inch across, contains many obscure symbolic references. The costumes of the women and the double ax suggest a Minoan religious influence.*

uppermost levels, Troy VIII was the Greek town where Alexander had paid homage to Achilles, and Troy IX, the top stratum, the level of the Roman town, with ornate public buildings. In his haste to find the city of the *Iliad*, Schliemann had raced right by it, ignoring the layer, VI, that archaeologists would later agree upon as the Troy of his dreams.

For the moment, most people accepted his gold-backed claims at face value. He was instantly famous, and he wrung every possible drop of acclaim from his discovery by corresponding with newspapers, giving lectures, and publishing several books on the subject. The gold was proof, to most scholars, that classical Greece did not burst out of a cultural vacuum. Indisputably, the Aegean had known wealth, splendor, and sophistication many centuries earlier.

Schliemann returned to Hissarlik frequently during the following years, and in 1878 he wrote that he had discovered "three small treasures and a large one of gold jewels." He then complained that, by the terms of his latest firman, "I had to give up two-thirds of all the objects I found to the Imperial Museum in Constantinople." In fact, whatever he may have surrendered to the Turks was a pittance compared with the king's ransom of some 9,074 items he had smuggled out of Turkey and would later donate to Germany. He displayed

25

his treasures at the palatial home he built in Athens.

Meanwhile, Schliemann's attention turned to the other side of the Aegean, where another worthy Homeric challenge lay—the fortress of Mycenae, overlooking the Argive plain in the Peloponnesus. This city was home to Agamemnon, who met a violent death there: According to legend, the king was murdered by his wife, Clytemnestra, and her lover, Aegisthus, when he returned from the Trojan War. Mycenae figured in many other tales, and its massive ruins—including walls built of huge stones, supposedly erected by the race of giants known as the Cyclopes—were regarded with awe in ancient times and had lured tourists and scholars ever since. In the second century AD, the Greek writer Pausanias had written that "Clytemnestra and Aegisthus were buried a little outside the wall, for they were not deemed worthy of burial within it, where Agamemnon lies and those who were murdered with him." Most scholars felt that the mention of Agamemnon's resting place referred not to Mycenae's main defensive wall but to the city walls instead.

Schliemann disagreed. In his usual style, he performed some quick, illegal excavations at Mycenae in 1874. The probes were fruitless, but he came back with a small army of diggers in 1876, this time with governmental approval in hand. Against all advice, he began searching for graves within the citadel. A few marvelous vases, knives, arrowheads, figurines, and other items turned up. Then, after a few weeks, he hit some tombstones. A circle of stone slabs surrounded them, forming a nearly continuous chain of benches and suggesting that this was Mycenae's public meeting place and sacred center. He pressed on at a furious pace.

For a time the earth clutched its secrets tightly. Finally, however, the diggers came upon a rectangular shaft leading down into the rock. It was a grave, the first of five, ranging in depth from three to 15 feet. Within these shafts lay the remains of 19 men, women, and children, all adorned with gold: The children were wrapped in burial shrouds into which were sewn gold-foil cutouts; the precious metal had also been fashioned into the breastplates and face masks that covered some of the men, while the women were bedecked with gold disks in the shape of bees, spirals, and octopuses. Weapons, gold

*A bust of Schliemann commissioned by Sophia stands watch over the couple's templelike mausoleum in Athens. The site of the tomb, chosen by Heinrich years before his death, provides views of both the Acropolis and the Aegean.*

drinking cups, brooches, pins, and other riches abounded. In sheer volume, this lode far exceeded the treasure that Schliemann had ascribed to Priam. Moreover, the artistry of these objects—the inlay work, the embossing, the stunning imagery of religious, hunting, or war scenes—was of a far higher quality than anything Schliemann had found at Troy. In the last of the shaft graves he uncovered a skeleton wearing the golden mask of a mustachioed and bearded prince *(cover)*. Schliemann was certain he recognized him. Recording this discovery, he wrote, "I have gazed on the face of Agamemnon."

Again, he was mistaken. On the basis of pottery styles and other clues, the shaft graves later proved to date from about 1600 BC, centuries before the assumed time of the Trojan War (1250 BC). Yet even Schliemann's severest critics could not deny the greatness of his achievement, for he had unearthed, not the early Greeks he had expected to find at Mycenae, but a previously unknown civilization. In the following years he extracted further proof of its wealth, artistry, and power at a number of other ruined citadels on the Greek mainland. Scholars subsequently named the new culture Mycenaean, after the legendary city of Agamemnon.

In the course of these digs and further efforts at Troy, Schliemann became a more skillful and careful archaeologist. In 1882 he took on as his associate Wilhelm Dörpfeld, a young architect who insisted upon a more meticulous field procedure. Dörpfeld would get the credit, in 1893, for defining Troy's nine layers and recognizing that Troy VI, not Troy II, was Homer's fabled city. But Schliemann himself, during the last years of his life, acknowledged seven layers and made plans for further exploration of the strata.

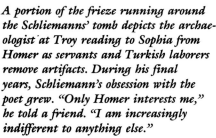

*A portion of the frieze running around the Schliemanns' tomb depicts the archaeologist at Troy reading to Sophia from Homer as servants and Turkish laborers remove artifacts. During his final years, Schliemann's obsession with the poet grew. "Only Homer interests me," he told a friend. "I am increasingly indifferent to anything else."*

Schliemann's death, in 1890 at the age of 68 of a brain inflammation after an ear operation, would leave the field to Dörpfeld. But Schliemann's own fame had grown with time, largely because of his prolific, if occasionally untrustworthy, writings. Messages honoring his memory poured into Athens. The king of Greece came to his mansion bearing wreaths. Upon the coffin were placed copies of the *Iliad* and the *Odyssey,* and at its head stood a pedestal bearing, like a presiding spirit, a bust of Homer.

For all Schliemann's faults, he had thrilled the world like no archaeologist before him. But he had a worthy successor on the Aegean stage, Sir Arthur Evans—English, rich, and gifted with the sort of energy that Schliemann possessed. He too would reveal the existence of an unknown and accomplished people—the Minoans, as he called them, after their legendary king, Minos. That ruler and his dominion had been mentioned in Homer's *Odyssey:* "Out in the dark blue seas there lies a land called Crete, a rich and lovely land, washed by the waves on every side, densely peopled and boasting ninety cities. . . . One of the ninety towns is a great city called Knossos, and there . . . King Minos ruled and enjoyed the friendship of almighty Zeus." Crete and Minos figured in various other legends, but the island kingdom was marginal to the Greeks' picture of their past, and

seemed purely mythic to later scholars. Not until Evans began his investigations would anyone suspect the astonishing truth—that Europe's first civilization had sprung from Cretan soil.

Arthur Evans had many advantages in his life and career. Born in 1851 in a Hertfordshire village, he grew up in a rambling, servant-filled house, received a first-rate education, and enjoyed a measure of financial security that was unknown to Schliemann as a youth. His father, John Evans, was not only an excellent businessman but also one of England's leading antiquarians. He had many scholarly friends and filled his house with ancient coins, Roman glass, Celtic weapons, and other bits of the past. Stimulated by this intellectual environment, Arthur, as a boy, accompanied his father on local digs.

His growing up was not without pains, however. His mother died when he was six, and his father soon remarried. When he entered Harrow, an elite public school, he was teased because of his extreme nearsightedness and short stature; his height as an adult was five feet two inches. Still, he was anything but a timid youth, full of self-confidence and possessing tremendous physical vigor.

After Harrow he attended Oxford, then Göttingen University in Germany. During the summers he traveled in the Balkans, a region that had long chafed under the yoke of the Ottoman Turks. Drawing on his travel experiences, he wrote a book about Bosnia and Herzegovina, and in 1877 took a job as the Balkan correspondent of the *Manchester Guardian*. As a journalist he proved highly opinionated; he was contemptuous of the Turks and fiercely supportive of Slavic nationalism. The dangers of this position did not concern him. Marrying the daughter of an Oxford historian in 1878, he took her to live in the city of Ragusa (present-day Dubrovnik). For the next five years he continued to send the *Guardian* reports of Ottoman iniquity and Slavic heroism. Finally the authorities acted, first throwing him in jail and ultimately expelling him from the country.

Fortunately, Evans had by now written a second book on the Balkans and was considered a capable historian. He took a job in 1884 as curator of Oxford's Ashmolean Museum—a neglected institution at the time. In the face of considerable opposition, Evans steered it into a new age, greatly adding to the collections, housing them in a new building, and transforming the Ashmolean into a world-famous museum during his quarter century of stewardship. The job allowed plenty of free time, which Evans did not waste. He found himself increasingly drawn to archaeology.

*Sir Arthur Evans* (left), **pioneer in the discovery of Minoan civilization, examines Mycenaean-style stirrup jars in Knossos around 1900. The British antiquarian devoted much of his life to the excavation and restoration of Knossos, illustrating and interpreting his discoveries in a monumental four-volume work,** The Palace of Minos. *Sealstones, the minutely carved objects that first drew Evans to Crete, are discussed in detail in his Volume II* (left, below).

In the spring and summer of 1883, he and his wife had toured Greece, visiting Mycenae and other prehistoric ruins and calling on Heinrich Schliemann in Athens. The Mycenaean treasures Schliemann had unearthed enthralled him, particularly the seals and signet rings—small objects, mostly of stone, that were used to press a design into wax or clay as an indication of authenticity. When inspecting these objects, Evans found that his extreme nearsightedness was an advantage: Because he had to bring the seals very close to see them at all, he could make out features that others had not noticed— pictures and symbols that seemed somehow not native to the Greek mainland. A minuscule image of an octopus suggested a maritime civilization; other designs looked somewhat Egyptian.

Over the next ten years, Evans lectured and wrote articles on many antiquarian subjects, while pondering a larger idea. Perhaps an advanced civilization had antedated the people who had poured treasure into the shaft graves at Mycenae and built great fortresses elsewhere on the Aegean mainland. If so, that civilization might have possessed some method of writing, perhaps akin to Egyptian hieroglyphs. "Throughout what is now the civilized European area, there must once have existed systems of picture writing such as still survive among the more primitive races of mankind," he wrote.

The sealstones were a hint. In 1893, while visiting Athens, Evans had occasion to see small, charmlike stones engraved with symbols that looked even more like hieroglyphs. The dealers told him that they came from Crete, the 160-mile-long, Turkish-controlled island that lay 65 miles south of the Greek mainland. Evans had heard of a large mound called Kephala, not far from the northern coast of Crete, where some huge storage jars had been dug up years earlier. Tradition identified this mound—several acres in area—as the site of Knossos, home of the legendary King Minos.

Schliemann had contemplated excavating Kephala. In a letter written in 1888, he declared: "I would like to end my life's labours with one great work—the prehistoric palace of the kings of Knossos in Crete." He even attempted to buy the mound from its Turkish owners, but, suspecting he was being cheated, called off negotiations. In 1894, Evans appropriated the dream. He purchased a share of the mound, in effect preventing anyone else from excavating it. War soon broke out between the Cretans and their Turkish overlords, and

*Evans, in white, with his associate Duncan Mackenzie and architect Christian Doll beside him, pauses for a picture on the palace's Grand Staircase, one of the most spectacular discoveries, as well as the greatest restoration problem, at Knossos. Workmen replaced burned and rotted timbers with iron girders and reinforced concrete in an undertaking Evans called "reconstitution" of the structure.*

Evans—vocally anti-Turk, as always—had to wait a few more years.

Fortunately for his plans, the Cretans won their freedom. By the year 1900 he was ready to dig. He was 48 years old, a widower without children. Seven years before, he had been shattered by the death of his wife from tuberculosis, and he would mourn her for the rest of his long life, writing all notes and letters on black-edged stationery. Knossos and Crete would be his passion.

From the start, Kephala-Knossos proved an archaeological marvel. Under his direction, 50 workmen—a force soon expanded to 180—began digging on March 23. Four days later, Evans wrote in his diary of the "extraordinary phenomenon" he was uncovering. He knew that he had hit upon a new civilization, and reasoned that it went "at least well back to a pre-Mycenaean period."

A few more days of work brought one of its people into view. On what seemed to be the floor level of a hall were two pieces of a fresco, a painting on fresh plaster. The fragments showed much of a life-size figure of a man holding a vase and wearing a distinctive loincloth that archaeologists had seen elsewhere: Men wearing exactly this garb were portrayed in paintings that adorned the tombs of ancient Egyptian nobles. The Egyptians depicted them bearing tribute to the pharaoh and identified them as Keftiu—"people of the islands." The Keftiu, Evans now speculated, must have been Cretans.

As the excavation proceeded, the maritime nature of this civilization became increasingly apparent. Pottery shards were decorated with images of octopuses, sea urchins, starfish, and dolphins. The trident, thought by some to be emblematic of sea power, was carved on walls, pillars, and seals. Although Egyptians had represented these islanders as paying tribute to Egypt, there could be no question that their power was great.

Interred in Kephala was an enormous palace that had been remodeled over a period of several centuries. On the west side of the mound, Evans discovered fresco fragments of what must have been a splendidly painted chamber. It was lined with stone benches, among which stood a high-backed stone chair with its seat at a level above the others. Evans wrote, "The elaborate decoration, the stately aloofness, superior size and elevation of the gypsum seat sufficiently declare it a throne-room." From this room, he was sure, King Minos—or rather, many kings, since he thought *minos* was probably a dynastic title rather than an individual's name—had ruled a great sea empire.

That first season of digging brought mysteries, as well. Images of bulls, which presumably had religious significance, appeared in a number of frescoes and reliefs; in certain of these scenes, a youth was shown somersaulting over the horns of a bull in some sort of game or ritual. Representations of females abounded, thought to be priestesses or deities. Sometimes they were depicted with doves or snakes, and frequently present was the double ax, a ubiquitous symbol of Minoan religion. Besides all these images, the excavators discovered hundreds of clay tablets inscribed with straight rows of picture writing—probably palace records. The hope of such a find was what had brought Evans to Knossos in the first place. He recognized that the written characters came in two forms, which he called Linear A and Linear B, but he was unable to decipher them—and would never succeed, despite decades of trying.

Still, the first year of digging had to be considered an unalloyed triumph. Between March and the cessation of activities in June, more than two acres of the site were uncovered. Evans had summoned a professional architect to help him fashion a general plan of the palace complex from indications of columns, doorways, staircases, ceilings, and floors. Knossos proved to have been a sprawling array of halls, corridors, ceremonial chambers, and other rooms, all surrounding an expansive paved court. Further digging would reveal that it had covered six acres and included some 1,400 rooms.

Evans was able to date the construction of the earliest palace by means of pottery and other artifacts. Finds such as Egyptian stone vases at Knossos, coupled with the discovery of lavishly decorated Minoan pottery in Egyptian tombs for which dates were known, indicated that the palace had been built in 1900 BC. Evans sank some test pits all the way down to virgin rock and found evidence of almost continuous settlement back to Stone Age days—perhaps as long ago as 8000 BC, he thought, although later testing would show that he was off by about two millennia.

The world was agog. These finds, wrote the *Times* of London, "equal, if they do not surpass, in importance the discoveries of Schliemann." Archaeologists rushed to Crete and began excavating other ruins, rapidly adding to the picture of the Minoans as a so-phisticated and potent society. Meanwhile, Evans kept digging, as productively as ever. A spectacular staircase was uncovered on the east side of the central courtyard in 1901. An inlaid gaming table appeared. More frescoes turned up, portraying religious rites and such decorative motifs as flowers and butterflies.

Year after year, Evans returned to explore the complex. Ever the plutocrat, he built a villa next to the site in 1906, stocked its cellars with fine wines, laid in foods from Fortnum and Mason in London, and entertained a stream of visitors. He devoted an appreciable frac-tion of his wealth not just to excavating Knossos but also to recon-structing it—restoring walls, floors, staircases, and columns. Al-though the actual walls had mostly been timber framed and the columns had also been wood, Evans used reinforced concrete exten-sively, taking care to match the appearance of the original as nearly as possible. He hired a gifted Swiss artist, Édouard Gilliéron, to piece together the fragments of frescoes and fill in the missing sections.

Archaeologists had never seen anything quite like these Cretan palaces, and they began to develop a theory of what they called palace-complexes—tightly administered economic communi-ties that testified to skills of governance every bit as impressive as the Minoan talents in architecture and engineering. In the works of art shone a love for nature and the sea, for sport and celebration, for luxury and pleasure. The Minoans were evidently a buoyant people, sensing no serious threat to their sunny existence. And indeed, their time of greatness was long. Evans worked out a timetable for Minoan civilization, beginning around 2500 BC and extending to about 1400 BC, when some unknown disaster ended their civilization.

He had strong suspicions about that disaster, however. Crete lies in an area of intense seismic activity, prey to earthquakes. During the course of his excavations, he noted that successive Knossos palaces had been damaged by tremors. A great fire had ravaged the last one, and many walls and ceilings had collapsed. He believed that a violent geological paroxysm had brought the Minoan world to ruin.

Between 1921 and 1935, Evans published four books on his findings. Bearing the collective title *The Palace of Minos,* they were written entirely with a quill pen. The last volume appeared when he was 84 years old. He had produced a scholarly masterpiece, but many questions about the Minoans remained to be answered, not least the problem of their relationship to other Aegean cultures. Evans was convinced that the magnificent accomplishments of classical Greece were rooted in the Minoan world and that the Mycenaeans had been a kind of semibarbaric interlude. Although they were great warriors, he considered Mycenaean culture to be derivative—"only a provincial variant" of Minoan civilization, in his dismissive phrase. He was wrong about this, as Schliemann had been wrong on some fundamental issues, and a new generation of archaeologists would dig up evidence to challenge this and other of his conclusions.

Sorting out the strands of Aegean history—the identity of the Mycenaeans, the fate of the Minoans, and the accomplishments of earlier Cycladic cultures—would provide plenty of work for the successors to Schliemann and Evans. The two giants had followed the trail of human progress back into darkness, back into unknown millennia, where they had found the light of human genius shining brighter than had ever been imagined. In the *Iliad,* Homer tells of how, after the victors left Troy to return home, the sea god Poseidon expunged every sign that humans had been there: "He made all smooth along the rip of the Hellespont and piled the endless beaches deep in sand again. . . ."

In their own very different ways, Schliemann and Evans had undone the work of Poseidon: They had removed the sands of time to show what the ancient Aegean once had been. And in their footsteps followed others who, one by one, laid bare the other sites of the realm's no longer forgotten civilizations.

# THE DIGGERS OF TROY

*I*t is no small irony that a 2,800-year-old allegorical poem about a war that may never have occurred, whose heroes are most likely fictional, and whose "author" may well have been several bards rather than a single individual inspired one of the greatest discoveries in the modern science of archaeology. The *Iliad* has been revered in Western culture since antiquity, but for centuries serious scholars viewed the work as an instructive parable with no basis in fact. In the 19th century, however, the so-called "romantic school" of archaeology rejected this interpretation. Heinrich Schliemann, a wealthy German entrepreneur and self-confessed romantic, became obsessed with proving the truth of Homer's tale.

In 1868 Schliemann visited Frank Calvert, an English expatriate living in Turkey, who led him to a hillock near his property. Calvert had probed the mound, called Hissarlik, and knew it to be man-

made. He convinced his guest that the site matched Homer's description, and Schliemann concluded that this was indeed Troy. Over the next 22 years, Schliemann directed seven major excavations at Hissarlik. He recruited his fellow countryman, Wilhelm Dörpfeld *(above, lower right)*, and Troy soon became Dörpfeld's overriding passion as well.

In the 1930s an American archaeologist, Carl Blegen, reopened the mound and conducted a more careful scientific examination. Still, Blegen, like his German predecessors, was a romantic. He accepted the "fundamental historicity" of the *Iliad* and went to Hissarlik looking for physical evidence to support it. Finally, in 1988, another German, Dr. Manfred Korfmann, arrived at Troy, this time with a different agenda and no preconceived notions. The saga of these four men—and the fate of the archaeological site that forever links them—is an epic in its own right.

# Heinrich Schliemann

## A MAN DRIVEN BY A BELIEF IN POETRY

Heinrich Schliemann was a complex man, motivated throughout the last 20 years of his life by one goal—to uncover Homer's fabled city of Troy. His methods, however, set off a storm of controversy that still rages. While some scholars regard him as the father of modern archaeology, others revile him for his reckless excavation of Hissarlik, condemning him for leaving the site a "ruin of a ruin."

Calvert had realized that there was not one Troy but several, built atop one another in layers. He counseled Schliemann to proceed slowly with small excavations, but the German ignored this advice in favor of a massive trench running right through the mound.

After three seasons of digging, Schliemann concluded that the next-to-lowest layer, Troy II *(below)*, was the "steep walled" city of the *Iliad*. Wilhelm Dörpfeld

joined him later and, inadvertently, helped disprove Schliemann's theory. In 1890 the two men discovered potsherds in the Troy VI level that dated from the Mycenaean period, the supposed time of the Trojan War. This convinced Dörpfeld that Troy VI was, in fact, the city they both sought. Schliemann ruminated alone in his tent for four days and then quietly said to Dörpfeld, "I think you are right." He made plans to return the next year to explore Troy VI further but died that winter. Ironically, his zealous uncovering of Troy II had destroyed much of the Troy VI layer above.

To reach the deepest level of Hissarlik, where he felt Homer's Troy must lie, Schliemann had his crew cut this great trench—measuring 131 feet long by 33 feet wide—into the face of the hill. Hundreds of tons of dirt and stone, containing untold evidence covering millennia of human habitation, were removed and unceremoniously dumped down the slope.

Thirty-six feet below ground level, Schliemann uncovered the remains of Troy II (left), finding gold and other treasures in this stratum. Troy II had been a wealthy, well-fortified citadel that showed signs of having been destroyed in a great conflagration, all of which matched Homer's description. Schliemann's error in naming this as the city ravaged in the Trojan War is excusable, given his incomplete grasp of Hissarlik's chronology.

# Wilhelm Dörpfeld

## MAKING SENSE OUT OF CHAOS

In 1882, Schliemann lured Dörpfeld away from an excavation at Olympia. Dörpfeld applied his skills as an architect to Hissarlik's complex stratigraphy, eventually identifying nine distinct layers.

After Schliemann's death in 1890, the digging stopped until 1893. Concentrating on the Troy VI level, Dörpfeld uncovered much of what had not been demolished by Schliemann, including sections of the walls (*below*). "Our master Schliemann would never have dared to hope that the walls of which Homer sang had been preserved to so great an extent," Dörpfeld wrote. He also found evidence that this city, much like Troy II, had met a violent end. Rather than trumpet his discovery as a repudiation of his late mentor's theory, Dörpfeld instead magnanimously concluded, "Schliemann has been vindicated."

*Members of Dörpfeld's work crew pose atop Hissarlik with the Trojan plain in the background. The height of the citadel above the surrounding flat countryside would have provided ample warning of an attack. During the time of Troy VI, the Dardanelles, known in ancient times as the Hellespont, lay a mile from the hill.*

# Carl Blegen

## WORKING WITH BRUSH RATHER THAN SHOVEL

The ravaged mound of Hissarlik lay undisturbed until 1932 when the American archaeologist Carl Blegen arrived, bringing a new, more conscientious approach. Blegen documented every step of the digging—which was now as likely to be done with a brush as with a shovel—on film. Focusing on the few remaining untouched areas *(opposite)*, he was able to subdivide Dörpfeld's nine principal layers into "no fewer than 46 strata," to which he assigned letters for identification. Scholars now had a detailed, unbroken record of human presence on Hissarlik for more than three millennia.

But Blegen's first priority was determining which level contained Homer's Troy. He concluded that Dörpfeld's choice, Troy VIh—the final substratum of the Sixth City—had been wrecked by an earthquake, not a Greek army. Dörpfeld, who visited the site in 1935, concurred.

In the next level, Troy VIIa, evidence pointed to a dramatic surge in population inside the city's walls, and there were large storage jars buried in the floors of houses *(below)*, indicative of a siege. Blegen also found a skeleton in this stratum that "looked rather as if the man had been struck down and left as he fell." Added to this were signs of widespread fire. "It is Settlement VIIa, then," wrote Blegen, "that must be recognized as the actual Troy, the ill-fated stronghold." But, despite his pronouncement, the matter was far from settled.

Schliemann and Dörpfeld intentionally left sections of Hissarlik intact to reflect its original height. Blegen dubbed one the Island and took the photo at left—with a man on top for scale—at the outset of his seven-year project. The Island yielded a wealth of data about Troy III, IV, and V—lesser-known settlements that have never been identified as the legendary city of the Iliad.

Two photos show the so-called Island during different stages of the excavation. Above, the layer containing Troy IV has been reached. Two years later, only the stump of the Island remains (left) after the walls of Troy III have been removed. Schliemann left another pinnacle (background), known as the Megaron, which sits within the foundation of a large building he identified as the palace of Troy II.

# Manfred Korfmann

# TROY VIEWED WITH FRESH EYES

One hundred years after Schliemann's death, Troy at last attracted an archaeologist who did not come seeking Homer in the ruins. "We are not proceeding from the *Iliad*; we proceed, rather, as prehistorians from this highly interesting crossroads of cultures," says Dr. Manfred Korfmann. Heading an international team of scholars, Korfmann plans a thorough 15-year reevaluation of Hissarlik with space-age technology, sophisticated computers, and aerial photographs *(right)*. Already the team has discovered a settlement below Troy I, which it calls Troy 0.

A critical portion of the project involves shoring up the sides of Schliemann's trench and stabilizing other exposed walls to prevent damage by the 300,000 tourists who now flock to the site each year. They, like the eminent scientists who preceded them, are lured by Troy's mystique.

Still, given the archaeological history of the site, Korfmann cannot avoid questions about Homer. Along with most scholars today, he has reverted to Dörpfeld's Troy VIh as the city of *the* Trojan War—if it ever took place. "I believe the *Iliad* contains a historical kernel of truth: that wars were constantly fought over this geopolitically important location, which controlled the straits and the approach to the Black Sea. The question of whether there ever was a Paris, or a Helen, must take a backseat."

*After removing a century's worth of accumulated detritus and vegetation from the great trench, workers construct a retaining wall to forestall further erosion. The goal is to restore the trench to the way it appeared during Schliemann's excavations as a monument to the history of archaeological research.*

# THE CITY BENEATH THE ASHES OF STRONGHYLE

**W**hile the dust raised by picks and hammer blows swirled around their heads, the quarry masters on the Aegean island of Santorini must have cursed silently at news of a discovery their workmen had made. Time was money. And they were not prepared to delay production, or sacrifice profits, for the sake of saving a few mysterious stone walls inconveniently poking up in the midst of the diggings.

The quarriers, as forward-looking 19th-century entrepreneurs, had no doubt where their own best interests lay. Their operation was a vital cog in the greatest engineering project of the day— the construction of the Suez Canal. The pumice they extracted from this small volcanic island—the southernmost of the Cyclades group, lying 70 miles north of Crete and 115 miles southeast of the nearest point on the Greek mainland—was an essential ingredient in the manufacture of a durable, seawater-resistant cement required by the canal builders for the new harbor installations at Port Said.

In January 1866, however, a few months after work on the Suez Canal project had begun, the long-dormant volcano that had created this abundant supply of pumice became active once again. Several French archaeologists and a group of Greek scientists arrived to observe the eruption and its effects at first hand. Inevitably, the walls so assiduously ignored by the quarry operators attracted the

*The cerulean waters of the Aegean now ripple above what was once the center of the ancient island of Thera, sunk under the sea—like the mythical Atlantis— by a huge volcanic blast more than 3,500 years ago.*

visitors' attention. A member of the Greek government's scientific mission examined the blocks, recognizing at once that they predated the deep blanket of pumice and ash spewed out by volcanic eruptions in ancient times.

The quarry operators, who did not share the official's excitement, continued their activities, indifferent to the likelihood that they were crushing valuable archaeological material into powder. Nevertheless, the landlord of the site—though apparently powerless to stop the quarrying—joined forces with a local doctor to conduct a small-scale excavation. Together they uncovered a house with several rooms and a collection of pottery fragments.

Intrigued by these finds, a French vulcanologist, Ferdinand Fouqué, enlisted the help of a local peasant, who pointed out ravines where antiquities had been found and showed Fouqué some of the discoveries he and his neighbors had made—a pair of golden rings and two small tombs, long since plundered. When he began to dig for himself, Fouqué found a crypt with a central pillar made of lava blocks, blades carved of the black volcanic glass known as obsidian, a human skeleton, and pieces of broken pottery, vividly decorated in patterns that resembled no known classical style.

Spurred by Fouqué's reports, a team of French scholars, Henrí Mamet and Henrí Gorcex, initiated their own, more formal excavation in 1870. They uncovered the remains of other buried houses, all solidly built and of considerable size, and found storage jars, their contents charred and blackened but still recognizable as barley, lentils, and peas.

Burrowing under a vineyard, they braved a passageway that led beneath a heap of pumice and loose gravel and found themselves confronting an extraordinary sight: walls covered with smooth white plaster and painted with highly realistic, vividly colored frescoes—in pale yellow, blood red, dark brown, and a blue of astonishing brilliance. But when they tried to dig away the volcanic debris piled against them, the frescoes crumbled. The archaeologists knew they had little time to survey this discovery—the gravel bank above their heads was clearly on the verge of collapse. Before the underground avalanche occurred, they managed to remove a substantial hoard of broken pottery. Once pieced together, the rescued fragments yielded one hundred vases, finely decorated in a completely unfamiliar style.

Neither Fouqué nor his compatriots were able to identify or date the makers of these objects and the buried buildings that had

Before Stronghyle vented its wrath on Thera in the second millennium BC, the island basked in the southern Aegean *(left, top)*. With the explosion, much of Stronghyle's interior was blown out and the surrounding walls collapsed. Seawater flooded the new basin, altering Thera's face *(middle)*. Over time, the northwestern section separated from the main portion, later called Santorini, to form the island Therasia *(bottom)*. Additional eruptions led to the formation of two other islands.

Until quite recently, scholars were virtually unanimous in the view that the eruption—which sent debris flying 20 miles high—occurred around 1500 BC. The Greek archaeologist Spyridon Marinatos, in particular, believed that the repercussions of this blast destroyed the Minoan civilization on nearby Crete. Others speculated that the explosion caused tidal waves that may explain the biblical account of the parting of the Red Sea. But no hard evidence supported these theories.

Analysis of ancient wood samples from as far away as Ireland and California does show, however, that trees were stunted in the 1620s BC—as a result perhaps of global cooling caused by an ash cloud. Samples from Greenland's ice also reveal high levels of acidity dating to 1645 BC, give or take 20 years, indicative of volcanic activity somewhere in the world. Clues suggesting a date earlier than the previously accepted 1500 BC have been found on Thera itself in the form of wood and seeds buried in the ash fall, carbon-dated to no later than 1600 BC.

housed them; Sir Arthur Evans's rediscovery of the Bronze Age civilization of Minoan Crete still lay 30 years in the future. The first excavators knew only that this mysterious people were the denizens of some remote era, unknown to modern scholars and unsung by the old Greek poets. Although a team of German archaeologists, led by Baron Hiller von Gaertringen, would do some digging on Santorini in the 1890s, a determined effort to investigate the riddle of the island and uncover the artistic glories buried deep beneath volcanic debris would not be made for nearly a hundred years.

When a serious and sustained excavation was made, the history of the ancient world had to be rewritten. The discovery helped fill in a vast blank space in the cultural history of the eastern Mediterranean, a hitherto unknown era one thousand years before the rise of classical Greece. Old notions, of barbarous islanders dozing in some kind of cultural torpor until jolted awake by Greek civilization's clarion call, proved to be far from the truth.

What lay hidden under Santorini's ash and pumice were the remains of a well-ordered and outward-looking society. Its members savored the blessings of peace and prosperity and left behind them positive proof of their creative energy, artistic talents, and sophisticated tastes. The inhabitants of Bronze Age Santorini, known in ancient times as Thera, enjoyed a level of material comfort that many communities today would envy.

On their sun-blessed, mountainous island, refreshed by cooling breezes redolent of wild herbs, the inhabitants of Thera built themselves a town of fine, tall houses. Behind their linteled doors lay well-proportioned rooms adorned with the finest examples of the fresco painter's art. From their windows and rooftops, the townspeople watched the traffic on the waters—fishermen carrying home the day's catch, neighbors from adjacent islands arriving to offer their wares for sale or barter, mariners bringing more exotic imports from distant shores.

In these pleasant surroundings, the islanders lived and grew increasingly rich, reaping the benefits of their fortunate position on the crossroads of the Aegean's most important trade routes. Their small homeland—barely four miles in width at its broadest point—was an important steppingstone for voyages between Crete, the Greek mainland, and the whole of the eastern Mediterranean. For generations they would enjoy unprecedented prosperity and an apparently unbroken peace.

This seemingly idyllic little world perched precariously on a geologic time bomb. Even today, the scattering of Aegean Islands, afloat in an azure sea, tricks the eye and lulls the mind into a false sense of peace. In fact, the geologic history of the area involves a series of cataclysms that began about a million years ago and may not even now be entirely ended.

The Aegean itself was born during an earthshaking spasm in the Pliocene epoch, five million years before the current era, when the waters of the Mediterranean Sea spilled over onto the Aegean landmass. In this upheaval, two great fragments of the planet's crust—the tectonic plates underlying the landmasses of Africa and Eurasia—rubbed and chafed against each other. Molten magma, welling up from the fissures where these plates met, blistered into numerous volcanoes, whose crests rose up out of the waters of the southern Aegean to form an array of islands between Turkey and the jagged peninsulas of mainland Greece. These volcanoes began erupting from the time of their birth; over the eons, most became inactive. But one in the southern Aegean—the ancients called it Stronghyle, "The Round One"—was far from extinct and would stir one day to menace the region's inhabitants.

It happened in the middle of the second millennium BC. A violent eruption blew apart Stronghyle, reducing Thera over time to three fragments—the main island of Santorini (known today by its ancient name of Thera), and the diminutive isles called Therasia and Aspronisi. (Today, two new landmasses—Nea Kameni and Palaea Kameni—are visible.) These remnants were left surrounding a great bay into which Stronghyle's ruptured cone had collapsed and were buried, some 200 feet deep, under layers of hot pumice and tephra— a thick, powdery volcanic ash.

Experts believe that a vast area was affected by the blast, not only along the Aegean but also around the Mediterranean shoreline and on the islands of its subsidiary seas. Depending on where they lived, people must have been shocked by the bangs, shaken by the earthquakes, terrified by the darkened skies or—according to the prevailing winds—choked by clouds of airborne ash and suffocated by poisonous gases.

Those who survived these events could not have forgotten them. In the view of some scholars, the memory of the horrors has

*Spyridon Marinatos—shown here inspecting a ceramic vessel decorated with Minoan motifs unearthed at ash-covered Akrotiri on Thera—marveled that the privilege had fallen to him "not of excavating the usual decayed ruin but of exploring a town abandoned and obliterated in the space of a few weeks."*

been preserved in myth: Images of volcanic catastrophe have found their way into the lore of Greece and places far beyond it. The Greek poet-chronicler Hesiod, in the eighth century BC, was the first known compiler of his people's ancient tales of the gods and their cosmic struggles. He described the terrible effects of combat between Zeus and the screaming monster Typhon, whose black tongues flickered from the mouths of his hundred snakes' heads while flames flashed from his multitudinous eyes. "And the heat from them both gripped the purple sea, the heat of thunder and lightning and of fire from such a monster, the heat of fiery storm winds and flaming thunderbolts," wrote Hesiod. "And the whole earth and firmament and sea boiled. And long waves spreading out in circles went seething over the headlands, and unquenchable earthquakes broke out."

Other Greek myths and legends spoke of entire islands that wandered aimlessly around the seas like ships adrift, perhaps a distorted reference to the chunks of foam-like pumice the volcano disgorged, which would have been light enough to float. Historians have also been intrigued by the Greek philosopher Plato's account of a lost continent called Atlantis, wondering if the tale of this doomed world—allegedly learned by the Athenian lawgiver Solon during a visit to Egypt's priests—might indeed have some kind of basis in fact. The story concerned a highly civilized society, one that could boast of achievements well in advance of its age, that sank beneath the waves in a single catastrophic night.

The vanished land, according to Plato's narrator, Critias, had been an island empire nourished by warm- and cold-water springs; its fertile plains yielded "every variety of food" in abundance, while its forests were luxuriant enough to support all manner of wildlife, including elephants. "Also," said Critias, "whatever fragrant things there now are in the earth, whether roots, or herbage, or woods, or essences which distill from fruit and flower, grew and thrived in that land . . . fair and wondrous and in infinite abundance."

The first inhabitants of Atlantis were the offspring of a union between a mortal woman and Poseidon, the god of the sea. They husbanded their natural resources wisely and built themselves a fine capital city containing great waterways spanned by handsome bridges, walls coated in precious metals, palaces glowing with stones in

variegated colors, and an ivory-roofed temple furnished with statues of gold. For centuries, peace and harmony prevailed within the kingdom, and ancient laws and customs were loyally honored. But this happy state came to an end when the base, human side of the Atlanteans' nature began to overpower the spark of divinity they had inherited from their immortal ancestor. They became corrupted with ambition, hungry for power, hypocrites hiding under a false shell.

So Zeus, father of all the gods, saw fit to punish them, and, wrote Plato, "There occurred violent earthquakes and floods, and in a single day and night of misfortune the island of Atlantis disappeared in the depths of the sea." Yet did the land sink completely? Did small islands remain? Whatever the distortions of the story, mutated through centuries of retelling, aspects of this tale roughly correspond to the geologic events occurring during the second-millennium eruption of Stronghyle.

*Tunneling under as much as 150 feet of volcanic ash and pumice, excavators at Akrotiri discovered great quantities of pottery vessels, like the freshly exposed stirrup jars shown above. Such passageways as the one pictured inset, which follows an unpaved Theran road, were erected to keep the ruins underground and thus protected from the elements. The danger of walls and ceilings collapsing eventually forced the archaeologists to make use of different methods.*

When in 1885 the peripatetic Victorian visitor James Theodore Bent arrived on Thera, which he called "this mysterious workshop of Vulcan," he responded with a thrill of horror to its lowering landscape, its black beaches, and its pervasive atmosphere of desolation, "fascinating in its hideousness." Bent's bleakly romantic picture of an empty wilderness, however, was not quite accurate. Besides the quarriers, still busily blasting away at the island's crust, there was a peasant community eking a living from the gray volcanic soil and resting in the shade of its own grapevines. When the first wave of excited 19th-century investigators had arrived, these local farmers had helped with the excavations. Small boys who had watched their fathers at the diggings and perhaps saw the dirt brushed gingerly from the earliest finds grew up to play a crucial role in the excavations undertaken in the 20th century.

*Sheltered beneath metal scaffolding and a molded fiberglass roof, the completely excavated West House—thought to be the residence of a wealthy sea captain—shows typical architectural features of the time, including a second story, a window beside the door, and a paved street in front.*

In the 1930s Spyridon Marinatos, a Greek archaeologist, became convinced that Thera's buried ruins held the answer to a mystery that had long puzzled scholars. In 1939 he published a paper putting forward his theory that the great Minoan palaces in Crete, and the empire over which they presided, had been destroyed by the same eruption that had ravaged Thera in the second millennium BC. He would cling to this theory throughout his life, although it has since been rejected by most archaeologists.

World War II, and the subsequent civil war in Greece, prevented Marinatos from testing this proposition in the field. He returned to Thera in 1958, shortly after an earthquake had struck the island, to examine its effects and perhaps find support for his thesis. Climbing a limestone ridge 1,200 feet high, he inspected ancient Greek and Roman ruins at the summit. But it was not until the 1960s, when he was appointed director general of the Greek Archaeological Service, that he was able to raise enough funds to launch a serious investigation.

Starting out as a professor of archaeology at the University of Athens, Marinatos had risen through the Greek Archaeological Service, becoming its Director of Antiquities and Monuments of Greece in 1956. Under its aegis he had excavated burial sites in Attica, discovered the remains of Minoan buildings at Amnisos and Vathypetro on Crete, and explored settlements and cemeteries of the Middle and Late Bronze Age in Messenia, on the mainland. Now he was in a position to establish a major excavation that would not only cap his career but would also satisfy Greek national pride; at the time, virtually all of the important digs in the Aegean were under the sponsorship of foreign organizations.

In 1965, Marinatos reconnoitered the island, calculating where to dig the first trench. He reasoned that the sunken mountain once had protected the southern coast from violent northwest winds. Here the village of Akrotiri, a picturesque town of little white houses and churches, sunswept all winter, offered, even in modern times, a safe harbor from storms.

By this time, the excavations carried out by the French led by Mamet in 1870 and by von Gaertringen's German team in the 1890s had almost entirely vanished under the plough. But by jiggling the childhood memories of certain elderly islanders, Marinatos was able to relocate the sites that had attracted his predecessors' interest. The old men led him to places in the environs of Akrotiri where the soil had subsided, apparently because of movements in ruins buried underneath, or where strange outcrops of stone suggested the presence of subterranean walls and doorways. In some places, he found donkeys drinking from circular stone water troughs that he recognized as massive prehistoric mortars.

After undertaking a detailed survey of this promising area, which produced maps and aerial photographs, Marinatos began to dig in the ravine that linked modern-day Akrotiri with the sea. Within a few hours of putting spade to soil, he began to uncover the remains of an ancient city.

It quickly became apparent that the buildings were often two or three floors high. Marinatos struggled over the logistics of excavating the structures without causing the partly collapsed walls of upper stories to cave in completely. The original builders had constructed their houses of rubble and clay, reinforced with timber. But the wood had burned out, and the clay had dried and crumbled; it was obvious to Marinatos that one good 20th-century rainstorm would transform the ruins into a pile of Bronze Age mud. His solution was to roof over the excavation site with corrugated sheet metal and fiberglass, which let in the sunlight. He supported this covering with a system of freestanding prefabricated steel girders. These protective structures were easy to assemble, expand, or move as work progressed.

To anchor the girders, the team dug pits down to bedrock. This procedure had the advantage of allowing the systematic probing of levels, revealing the history of the site. Exploratory tunnels were extended through the pumice and ash to locate remains. Soil, rock, and debris were also removed from above the remains to open up large areas for study.

Where wooden supporting beams and lintels had disintegrated, leaving only hollow imprints in the enclosing shell of pumice, cement was poured into these gaps. As it set, the concrete adhered to the surfaces of the surviving masonry and molded itself into the shapes of the missing pieces of timber, ensuring that the structures would remain intact. When such architectural remains were found, portable roofs were set up over them to protect them.

As Marinatos went on to uncover and initiate the exploration of 10 whole buildings, he often discarded conventional methods. He did not, for example, follow any single system in naming the buildings. He labeled four according to the first letters of the Greek alphabet—alpha, beta, gamma, delta. Others were designated by their building material and were called Xesté—the Greek term for the dressed stone blocks known as ashlars—numbers 1 through 4. Confusingly, Arabic numerals were used both to distinguish between the various Xesté houses and to identify individual rooms. The two last buildings were named for certain distinctive features—the House of the Ladies for its wall painting of women in Minoan dress, and the West House for its location.

Marinatos speculated as to the likely identity of the houses' original occupants. West House, which contained frescoes on nautical themes, must, in Marinatos's view, have belonged to an important naval man—perhaps the admiral of the Theran fleet—or to an entire dynasty of sea captains. In Alpha House he identified one

*This cast of a 15-inch-high wooden tripod table—formed by pouring plaster into a cavity left by the piece after it disintegrated in hardened volcanic debris—comes from Akrotiri's Delta building. While wood decomposed over the eons, some wicker and rush baskets survived, though in powdered condition.*

*Volcanic ash and debris in the Delta building preserved the Spring Fresco, pottery vessels and shards, and the shape of a bed that itself had long since decayed. By forcing plaster into the cavity left by the bed, restorer Stamatis Perrakis (right) obtained a cast of remarkable detail, showing even the thongs used to bind the frame. The reproduction above, which measures a little more than five feet long and two feet wide, recreates the original wood frame and probable hide covering.*

small, self-contained enclosure, opening off a corridor, as a porter's lodge. And when the excavators uncovered what was obviously a street running between several buildings, Marinatos allowed himself a particularly fanciful form of nomenclature. One of the adjoining houses had yielded some artisans' tools; the director therefore named the road after the Telchines—nine dog-headed, flippered monsters, offspring of a goddess of the sea, who, according to an ancient myth, had taught the useful arts to humankind.

While Marinatos excavated, his wife and 17-year-old daughter Nanno lived with him in a large, comfortable villa built around a courtyard overlooking the site. The building, with its adjoining workrooms, could house as many as 20 people, and his assistants also lived there. Nanno had accompanied her father on digs from the time she was five, when Marinatos would, on occasion, plant newfound objects—a ring or a pendant, for example—close to the surface of the soil, where the child could have the pleasure of finding it and announcing her discovery to all present. Such early encouragement bore fruit, for Nanno would grow up to become a distinguished archaeologist in her own right.

From the moment he realized the significance of his find, Marinatos "was on a high that had no equal," his daughter recalls. "There began a hurricane of hyperactivity," she later reported. "The focus of the storm was on the south shore of Thera, and the eye of the storm was Spyridon Marinatos."

55

Demanding of his subordinates, Marinatos was not an easy man to work with. Although constantly dreaming up new concepts, he sometimes resisted those of his associates, who found that the easiest way to get an idea accepted was to "remind" Marinatos that he had thought of the notion himself a few days earlier. And those around him knew that when reporters and television cameramen showed up, they had best be immediately directed to the excavation's top archaeologist. When a delicate operation was necessary to bring forth from the earth a fragment of fresco, the workers would first try to direct Marinatos's attention elsewhere. Otherwise they might be subjected to a stream of needless injunctions to take care, nervously barked at them by their frantic director.

Endowed with that brand of imagination that had led Schliemann to the Aegean realms, Marinatos too saw, wherever the situation warranted, an ancient Greek myth come to life. And like his predecessor, he was under the spell of Homer. Whenever he set sail, he liked to imagine himself accompanied by Odysseus, the hero of Homer's *Odyssey,* and about to encounter similar adventures. His daughter remembers long evenings at the site, under the spell of his storytelling, which included both tales invented on the spot and re-created Homeric episodes.

Marinatos's creative thinking served him in practical circumstances as well. When a farmer showed him the salty ground water and beach sand he had found when digging a well, Marinatos immediately saw, in his mind's eye, ships and a harbor beneath the farm. He knew that the volcanic eruption that had ruptured the island had extended its shores with rubble and ash, but until that moment he had had no clues as to where the original coastline had been.

From the very beginning of the project the finds were abundant and impressive, yielding thousands of domestic implements, stone tools, pottery, and traces of broken furniture. Then, in September 1968, during the second season of excavation, Marinatos made a truly spectacular discovery—the colored fragments of a beautifully executed wall painting depicting the head of a man, several large blue birds in flight, and a monkey's head, also blue. Writing up the find in his journal, Marinatos pondered the meaning of the images. Was the original scene a formidably ancient representation of a well-known Greek myth? "I begin to wonder if it is Orpheus or Thamyris

*An upper-level bathroom in the West House still contains two benches divided by a four-inch slit that channeled waste through clay pipes to sewers beneath the street. In the vacant space to the left of the toilets may have once stood a bathtub made of fired clay, along with a three-legged vessel for pouring the water.*

with a lyre, having in front of him all the birds of the forest," he wrote.

Whatever tale the painter meant to tell, the discovery of the fresco of birds and monkey was only the beginning. Fresh examples of Theran art, incomplete but often in a remarkably good state of preservation, came to light. Working with soft brushes among fresco fragments, whisking away the dust of time, meant, of course, that progress would be tortoiselike. The team excavating the West House, for example, sometimes crept at the rate of one inch a day through a single square yard of ash.

In another chamber, the team found a wall painting showing a band of blue monkeys scrambling over a mass of rock that bore a striking resemblance to the landscape close to the excavation site. The people of Akrotiri, it now became evident, had lived in rooms that glowed with lovingly detailed frescoes full of the symbolism that was part of their daily and ritual lives.

One of the most electrifying discoveries came in 1970: In a large room in the building known as Delta, a wall fresco still stood in its original position, perfectly intact. Most of the wall paintings Marinatos had unearthed up to this point lay in fragments; a few still sat, precariously, in place, but were no longer anchored to the walls. It is likely that many had been damaged when the earth tremors rocked the island; others had suffered in more recent times, when floodwaters penetrated parts of the buried town. But, miraculously, the work of art in the Delta building revealed itself in its original splendor, positioned where its previous owners had last gazed upon it.

The British archaeologist Colin Renfrew was present when the fresco was exposed. "We all realized," he recalls, "that here was one of the most perfect works of art to have been preserved for us from prehistoric times."

Christos Doumas—second-in-command to Marinatos at the time and later the project's director—describes the highly charged atmosphere as the picture emerged from its coating of debris: "The slow process of removing the volcanic ash with a brush, and the gradual revelation, inch by inch, of this magnificent work of art, kept us in a state of continuous excitement for weeks." The painting, which its finders named *The Coming of Spring,* showed swallows—depicted with vivid naturalism by someone with a keen eye for the flight patterns and behavior of these birds—moving through a Theran landscape of lilies and multicolored rocks. It was a frozen moment in past time, shedding light on a lost world. Marinatos suggested that scientists might find the scene an invaluable source of information on the island's geologic features before Stronghyle's outburst. As for the swallows, Marinatos asserted that they probably had never returned to this particular island, although today they live on all the surrounding ones. He wondered what internal mechanism might have recoded their migrating habits, perpetually warning them away from Thera.

The thrill of discovery soon gave way to the realization that the wall that held the image was in such poor condition that it might crumble at any moment. Marinatos called together the country's three greatest experts in the restoration of ancient art. The specialists closeted themselves in a 48-hour-long emergency meeting on site, agonizing over the urgent measures necessary to rescue the fresco in time, while facing the risk that any miscalculation on their part might lead to its total destruction.

Their only hope was to separate and remove the painted surface from the underlying wall as if it were a second skin. This operation was complex, delicate, and fraught with suspense at every step. First, to hold the painting together and keep it from collapsing, the conservators covered the whole of its face with a sheet of gauze soaked in an adhesive and topped by a layer of heavier, stronger fabric. Starting from the bottom of the fresco, they then glued to the layer of fabric a series of vertical straps, leaving the ends free at the top. The next step was to fix these strap ends securely to a horizontal beam fastened to the wall above the fresco. The fresco could thereby be kept intact, suspended from the beam, while the process of removing it took place.

The restorers made a polystyrene mold of the fabric-covered wall that bore the fresco, thus ensuring that any irregularities in the surface would be reproduced in the mold. Then, using long steel needles designed specifically for this task, the master restorer Stamatis Perrakis began to prize away, from the wall beneath, the layer of plaster that held the fresco. Once detached, the fresco—together with its wrappings, the supporting beam, and the mold into which it was now fitted, was lowered with excruciating slowness until it lay face-

# MYSTERIOUS FIGURES OF MARBLE
# EVOKING A FORGOTTEN PAST

When early 19th-century European travelers to the Aegean first brought back with them marble relics they regarded as primitive curiosities, no one imagined that the pieces predated classical Greece. Not until the further development of archaeological methods decades later were the carvings traced to a vigorous culture that flourished on the Cyclades between 3500 and 2000 BC.

The British investigator James Theodore Bent was the first to carry out systematic excavations on the Cyclades (Greek for "those in a circle," which reflects the islands' position around Apollo's shrine on the sacred isle of Delos). Bent's finds in the 1880s led him to posit the existence of "a vast, prehistoric empire." Others curious about the culture followed, including the pioneering Greek archaeologist Christos Tsountas. He was struck by the society's accomplishments, evidenced by the marble vases and figures, decorative ceramic bowls, and silver jewelry that he dug from the ground, and by its ability to make bronze tools and weapons. The stylized figures, with their backward-tilting heads, were particularly eye-catching. Predominantly female, they ranged from barely two inches tall to almost life-size.

The beginnings of the culture, however, were hard to pin down. Then, in 1949, another Greek archaeologist, Nikolaos Kontoleon, uncovered an early cultural center on the island of Grotta. Eleven years later, British and American researchers had unearthed Stone Age settlements on Saliagos and Keros. As society evolved on the Cyclades and wealth grew through trade in minerals, the dead went increasingly to their graves accompanied by various objects, including obsidian blades like those shown above together with the cores from which they came. But chief among the burial goods were the figures, largely produced with stone tools ranging from emery for carving to obsidian for incising details and scraping surfaces smooth.

Showing signs of wear and even of repair, the figures were probably used by their owners during their lifetimes, possibly as votive objects. Traces of color suggest that many apparently were painted. Since female figures predominate, some scholars think they may represent a goddess important to the islanders.

*A spare, austere style suggestive of modern art characterizes Cycladic sculpture. This marble head, found on the island of Amorgos, dates from the high point of the culture, approximately 2700 to 2400 BC.*

Superimposed against a backdrop of a marble quarry on the island of Naxos is the headless Fat Lady of Saliagos (below), carved about 4000 BC. Some researchers speculate that this Neolithic figure, measuring approximately 2¼ inches long, and its successors may have represented a fertility goddess or other deity.

The best known of the island art forms is the folded-arm, canonical figure, so called because it conforms to rigid conventions. This one (right), made in Naxos sometime between 2600 and 2400 BC, has the tapered head, incised pubic triangle, pointed feet, and folded arms that are characteristic of the form.

Tiny "violin figurines," pared-down abstractions of the human form like this five-inch example at left, denote the first phase (3200-2700 BC) of early Cycladic culture. The presence of such white marble figures in some, but not most, stone-slab graves is believed to reflect the high status of the occupants.

Squared off and flattened, a late version of the folded-arm pose from about 2500 to 2200 BC (right) signals the beginning of a decline in marble carving. Anatomical features are disproportionate, and the left arm is positioned, atypically, under the right.

A harpist (2700-2500 BC), from a grave on Keros (below), is among the most complex sculptures found. Dating the piece is difficult because it was illegally excavated and sold before being properly studied.

The belt across his chest and the dagger in his hand mark the figure below as a warrior-hunter. Such military pieces, dating from 2400 to 2200 BC, were the last figures to be produced by a culture on the brink of turmoil and extinction.

down on the floor. Finally, a second polystyrene mold, this time of the wall that had supported the fresco, was created, and was carefully placed over the exposed back side of the fresco. Safely sandwiched between both of them, the treasure was safely transported for restoration to the workshop and housing complex that had been built in Akrotiri. There a solvent was used to remove the fabric covering without damaging the painting.

Even shattered paintings could be reassembled. After meticulously copying each fragment and precisely recording its original position, the restorers would treat the pieces with acetone and diluted epoxy resin to remove destructive moisture and protect the colors. They then covered these in gauze and transferred them to the laboratory to be cleaned and analyzed. By systematic reassembly— plus the sort of imaginative agility needed to solve jigsaw puzzles of monumental complexity—the almost-lost artworks were gradually returned to something approximating their original integrity. To complete each work, however, took several years, with as many as a dozen experts at a time working on the frescoes.

The archaeologists and conservators were soon joined by specialists in various disciplines—geologists, metallurgists, zoologists, botanists, and many others. Through their attentions, the buried town began to emerge from its long sleep. One thing was clear even from the tantalizing fresco fragments: The vanished inhabitants of Thera had been a gifted and creative people, endowed with artistic talents and a lively appreciation of their fruits.

It did not take these investigators long to confirm that the town had been a place of consequence. A traveler landing at the port would have been impressed by the ranks of lofty buildings rising above the shoreline. The island of Thera might have been of only modest size, but its port was—by the standard of its age—a sprawling metropolis, possibly covering 31 acres.

Large, solidly built houses rose two, three, or perhaps four stories high. These may have been the commodious homes of individual families, or communal dwellings, designed to fit as many people as possible into a limited space. In its density, the settlement anticipated the teeming European seaports of the Middle Ages. It was a labyrinth of narrow, twisting streets—barely wide enough for a pack animal's passage—debouching into small, oddly shaped squares, from which dark alleyways lurched off in all directions. Inside this maze, the inhabitants enjoyed a high standard of living.

*Called pithoi, these large pottery jars, discovered in a storage room at the northern end of the Akrotiri excavations, once contained wine, grain, and olive oil, which would have been imported from Crete and the mainland of Greece to supplement local supplies. The broken base of another vessel still holds snail shells (right), the remains of what must have been a succulent treat for the Therans.*

Their homes were fitted out with substantial doors and staircases; light from large windows flooded their generously proportioned rooms. The wooden furniture within these chambers has long since perished, but the ghost outlines of tables, beds, and stools remain, imprinted upon the blanket of volcanic ash. Plaster casts, made from these impressions, reveal elegant shapes and fine detail.

Besides having a penchant for comfort and an eye for good design, the Therans appreciated personal cleanliness. Their houses boasted bathrooms equipped with terra-cotta tubs and stone toilets that once may have had wooden seats. The toilets were found on the second stories of the buildings and were linked, through clay pipes embedded in the thickness of the walls, to a sophisticated communal drainage system that ran beneath the streets.

No discoveries have yet been made that indicate the presence of any palace-dwelling monarch, but whatever their mode of government, the Therans must have possessed some form of centralized civic authority. Public works, such as the sewers carrying away the waste from private houses, as well as the presence of well-maintained pavements, testify to the success of a group or an individual in marshaling resources and making decisions for the common good.

Fishermen's nets, supplemented by the crops and herds of landward farms, kept the community well nourished. In addition, every house had its mill for grinding barley flour to make bread and storage cupboards stocked with almonds and pistachios. Surviving cattle bones rarely show marks of the slaughterer's ax, leading to the conclusion that farmers kept them as beasts of burden and as sources of milk and cheese. The favored meats included mutton, lamb, goat, pork, and various types of furred or feathered game. At that time, wild boar no longer roamed the Theran wilderness, but their tusks, found in abundance, indicate that off-island hunters found a ready market at Akrotiri for either the carcasses or the tusks, which may have been used in decorating helmets.

Native grapes may have sufficed to fill the island's wine jars and fruit bowls, but the foreign vessels in which olives were recovered suggest that they and their oil came in from other islands. Large storage jars,

63

believed to be of Syro-Palestinian origin, are evidence of trade with the Near East or Egypt. The volume of seashells found among the ruins indicates that mollusks, especially the members of one particularly succulent species of snails that had to be imported from Crete, were a popular delicacy, as were limpets and the briny flesh scooped from sea-urchin casings. "A Bronze Age feast," Marinatos called these gustatory discoveries.

To pay for such imports, Thera obviously had to produce exportable wealth of her own. This may well have been in the form of such perishable products as saffron, wine, and honey, or of such intangible goods as seamanship and navigational skill, with Theran mariners earning their living through the burgeoning commercial traffic, ferrying goods around their native Aegean waters and possibly farther afield.

Akrotiri would have been a hive of industry, turning out products for both home consumption and foreign trade. Every building displayed signs of its occupants' productivity—a workshop, a storehouse, a supply of tools, heaps of crushed murex shells that might have been used in the production of purple dye. The houses must have hummed with the rhythms of women weaving; the clay weights for their looms have turned up in the remains of virtually every home on the site. So too has evidence of a thriving stoneware industry on a scale that suggests an export trade; distinctive three-legged mortars made of Theran porphyrite, a gray rock with white crystals, have been found in large quantities on Crete.

In addition to working with this native material, Theran stone carvers imported enormous quantities of obsidian from the island of Melos, the Aegean's most important source of this glassy, black volcanic rock, which was in demand for forming into sharp-edged instruments and was probably far cheaper than bronze. Yet bronze vases have been found on Thera and appear, by their design, to have come either from Crete or from mainland Greece. Also, metalworkers imported silver-bearing lead, most likely from the mines at Laurion, on the mainland, or perhaps from sources in the Cyclades, for refining in Theran workshops.

Although their kilns have not yet been located, Theran potters turned out vast quantities of ceramic vessels, made either from the coarse-textured, buff-coloured local clay or from imported materials with a different mineral content. More than 50 different types of pots—cookware, incense burners, fruit stands, ewers, jugs, drinking

*Discovered in a Cycladic grave on Naxos, these lead models of longboats—the largest of which is almost 16 inches in length—reveal how ancient mariners navigated the Aegean. The obsidian of Melos, seen below in its raw state, drew many such boats to its shores.*

# MELOS: THE OBSIDIAN CONNECTION

As long ago as 10,000 BC, seafarers across the Aegean traveled to the island of Melos, 50 miles northwest of Thera, in pursuit of the black volcanic glass known as obsidian. Valued for its sharpness and durability as well as its availability, obsidian provided an excellent cutting edge for tools and weapons eons before metals came into use for this purpose.

A characteristic molecular "signature" common to most samples pinpoints Melos as the almost-exclusive source for the obsidian discovered throughout the Aegean area. Although scant hard evidence exists, scholars generally believe that during the Early Bronze Age the inhabitants of Melos did not exploit this rich resource by asserting ownership rights and developing a lucrative trade with the mainland, Crete, and the other islands in the Cyclades. Rather, it would seem that

sailors and traders simply appeared on Melian shores, ventured to the quarries, and helped themselves, using crude tools to pry it from its rocky matrix. Back home, they kept what they needed and traded the surplus for various goods and raw materials.

During this period, seafaring voyagers of the region apparently traveled to Melos in narrow craft called longships *(left, top)* small models of which have been discovered on Naxos,

an island to the north of Thera and east of Melos. Until around 1800 BC, when sails advanced the art of seamanship, the sleek vessels were powered solely by a crew of oarsmen, believed to have numbered as many as 50 or as few as 25. Loaded with food rations, primitive equipment, and any other essentials—and retaining space for the haul—the sleek longships could probably cover up to 200 miles in a round-trip journey that might last two weeks.

*One of the larger islands among the Cyclades, obsidian-rich Melos was situated in the Aegean within longboat range—roughly 100 miles—of nearly all of the other islands, including Thera and Naxos. Probably through trade, Melian obsidian reached such far-flung locations as present-day Greece just south of the Bulgarian border and western Turkey.*

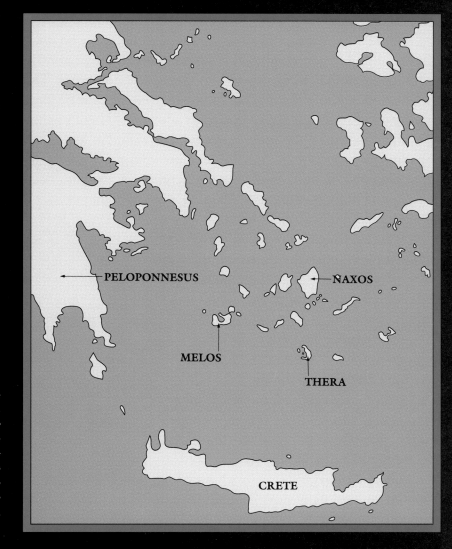

PELOPONNESUS

NAXOS

MELOS

THERA

CRETE

cups, storage jars, and artifacts apparently for some unknown ritual function—have been recovered. Except for the most practical braziers and cookpots, few lacked decoration. Every meal brought forth a blaze of color: Basins, cups, and jugs were painted with crocuses and lilies, ears of barley, birds in flight, fishes darting through a ceramic sea. Not all these wares came from island potteries; a multitude of Cretan vases have turned up at Akrotiri.

The reason behind this profusion of pottery from Crete is hardly mysterious. The influence of Minoan Crete, either by cultural persuasion or by political influence, was conspicuous throughout the southern Aegean by the second millennium BC. And nowhere is the evidence of the mingling of Minoan and native Cycladic cultures more powerful than in the rediscovered world of Bronze Age Thera.

The townscape itself, with its jumble of flat-roofed houses packed into narrow streets, would have made a Cretan traveler feel at home. Inside these buildings certain architectural features, such as a window beside each doorway, suggest that local artisans followed traditions similar to those of their Cretan counterparts. The artists who covered the walls of Theran rooms with vibrant frescoes used the same techniques as Cretan painters, although Theran painting was more marked by the individual styles of different artists. In the shops and warehouses of Akrotiri, traders sold their goods according to the Minoan system of measurement; the scales they used are missing, but their lead balance weights—of the same sizes and values as those found on Crete—remain.

However strong the Minoan connection, Thera was more than a mere cultural suburb of Crete. The Mycenaean culture, rising to power on the Greek mainland, had also begun to make its presence felt on the islands. Indeed, some scholars suggest that the seafarers of the Cyclades may have built and steered the ships that first brought the men of Mycenae into the Aegean. Whatever the nature of this traffic, neither mainlanders nor islanders remained unaffected. Influences and objects must have flowed in both directions. Pottery of mainland design is found on Thera; jugs of provable Cycladic origin have turned up in Mycenae. A pair of gold ear-

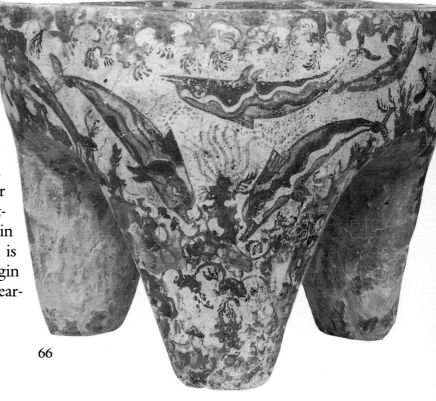

*Made from an ostrich egg, the ceremonial container at left, called a rhyton, has a neck and base of faience, or glazed earthenware. Since ostriches were not native to Thera, the piece, found in the Delta building, was probably Egyptian.*

*This bathtub-shaped container, called a* kymbe *by Marinatos, is a rare form found nowhere in the Aegean except Thera. Its surface is decorated with papyrus-like plants and chamois, animals pictured only on these kymbe vessels.*

*Found on a window sill in the West House, this stone offering table—standing just 11½ inches high—is decorated in painted stucco with dolphins and other marine motifs (left). The painting style is similar to that seen in Thera's frescoes.*

rings uncovered in the shaft graves at Mycenae exactly matches those dangling from the ears of a maiden gathering saffron in a wall painting at Akrotiri.

If the Therans learned the art of writing from their Minoan neighbors, no proof has yet been found. Only a few broken bits of pottery, probably imported, display markings in the Cretan script known as Linear A. Archaeologists exploring the remnants of ancient cultures that have left no written texts are accustomed to describe such sites as silent. But in their miraculously preserved wall paintings, the Therans speak volumes. The meanings of many images may be inaccessible, the nuances of belief and custom lost to the world forever, but the scenes their artists created enable us to glimpse the world they saw: Flowers are reproduced in loving detail, wild and domestic creatures play in gardens, boys box one another, birds dart among the flowers, ships visit unknown ports, and a girl pauses while gathering crocuses to nurse an injured foot.

In Theran art, and probably in Theran lives, rites and ceremonies played a crucial part. One fresco shows a procession ascending a rocky hilltop to conduct some ritual, perhaps to a pastoral deity, as shepherds tend their flocks nearby. In another, women gather the stamens of saffron crocuses and offer them up to an enthroned female figure— much larger than the others, almost certainly a goddess. She is flanked by an exotic beast not found on Thera—a monkey—and one imaginary creature, the fantastical creature known as the griffin.

No goddess, however potent, could protect the Therans from the catastrophe that destroyed their island. Yet while the islanders lost their homes, the absence of human skeletons or precious objects suggests that most probably managed to escape in time. Earthquakes rocked the island, no doubt months before the mountain exploded, but they may not have been recognized as the harbingers of the great horror to come. After they were over, some islanders felt safe enough to start repairing their damaged houses. Excavators have found evidence of abortive rebuilding attempts. Boulders, notched to hold the ropes slung around them, apparently served as wrecking balls to knock down unsafe structures. In one room the excavators came upon workmen's bowls, still filled with plaster ready to be spread on reassembled walls.

But at some point the reconstruction projects stopped dead. People must have sensed that something momentous was about to happen, perhaps warned by threads of smoke from the mountain's cone and by the fumes of dangerous gases that wafted into the city. When the call to evacuate the island came, artisans downed tools and left both their raw materials and a number of half-finished articles behind them. Few metal objects remain, perhaps because they were still so highly prized, as well as light to carry. Gathering their most precious belongings, rejecting only those goods too bulky or too inconsequential to carry such as pottery, and setting aside some storage jars filled with foodstuffs against the day of their hoped-for return, the Therans apparently boarded their ships and sailed to some unknown place of safety.

Thera did not stay uninhabited forever. Within a few centuries, people returned and built themselves new homes on or near the ash-covered sites deserted by their predecessors. The fifth-century BC Greek historian Herodotus recounted a legend, which was ancient even in his time, to account for Thera's absorption into the Grecian world. When the Olympian god Zeus transformed himself into a bull and carried off the maiden Europa, her mother and brothers left the land called Phoenicia to seek her among the islands. One brother, Cadmus, combing the Aegean, paused on Thera in his search, built a shrine there to the sea god Poseidon, and left some of his Phoenician comrades and kinsmen behind. Presumably the island was not entirely devoid of female inhabitants, for these castaways managed to reproduce themselves and flourish there for eight generations, until mainland Greeks from Sparta came and claimed the island for their own.

In whatever manner the newcomers arrived, their descendants felt the hot breath of the old volcano. The Greek historian Strabo described the effects of an eruption that took place in 197 BC, pushing up a new islet from its subterranean furnaces far beneath the floor of Thera's bay. "Between Thera and Therasia fires broke forth from the sea," he wrote, "and continued for four days, so that the whole sea boiled and blazed, and the fires cast up an island, which was gradually elevated as though by levers, and consisted of burning masses." This tiny isle is known today as Palaea Kameni.

Such upheavals continued into modern times. An eruption in

1650 shot flames into the air that could be seen as far away as Herakleion in Crete, where the tidal waves engendered by the blast swept away the ships of a Turkish invasion fleet. Between 1866 and 1950, five periods of volcanic activity caused new clusters of rock to emerge, sink, rise again, and fuse into a single new island—Nea Kameni. And scalding vapors still seep from the vents of the new volcano that formed on Thera after the ancient eruption.

Marinatos's passionate dedication to resurrecting the ancient city had tragic consequences for him. In 1974, while supervising the installation of a new mechanism for removing ash from the site, he stepped onto a wall and began frantically shouting out instructions and warnings to his crew. Suddenly he doubled over in pain and fell; an artery in his head had burst, and he died from the combination of fall and stroke. His life ended near the spot where he had first set spade to soil. In line with his wishes, conveyed by his wife, he was buried in Room 16 of the Delta building, where a thick layer of pumice had fallen in through open windows at the time of the eruption. In excavating this ground-floor room, Marinatos had found two drinking cups made from ostrich eggs and decorated with colored glazes similar to ones used in Egypt, which he believed indicated some kind of contact between Thera and the land of the pharaohs.

A multitude of specialists would continue the probing of Thera, but two, in particular, would feel Marinatos's influence in subsequent years, even as they took the work in new directions. Christos Doumas, who had assisted him for so long, took over as director of the dig, and Marinatos's daughter Nanno, who was 24 when he died, became a world-recognized specialist in analyzing Theran frescoes. "When my father found a fleet of ships painted on the walls of West House, he interpreted them as a glimpse into some historic voyage," Nanno Marinatos recalled. "But as I studied the frescoes I began to see them differently. My attention was drawn in particular to such things as streamers of flowers shown draped from the rigging. To me it was not a voyage at all, but a religious celebration on the Ae-

*Burdened by the huge weight of ash that blanketed Thera in its distant past, this stone staircase in the northern section of the Delta building collapsed on what was once its sturdy timber frame. Partly excavated, the steps tantalize archaeologists with hints of what may lie immediately beyond and in the rest of the still-uncovered remains of Akrotiri.*

gean, perhaps a tribute to a Minoan deity of the sea. That is the intriguing part of my relationship with my father. He influenced me so much, and yet I have often come to conclusions opposite to his."

The site remains a fertile ground for exploration; in fact, the ancient town's borders are still unknown. Excavations since Marinatos's death have revealed more houses in an area extending over 11,000 square yards, and similar ruins have been found a mile to the west and a quarter mile east of the dig.

Marinatos himself maintained that it would take not merely years but centuries to uncover and interpret all the material awaiting attention in this trove of archaeological treasures. Doumas has estimated that "the material produced by this site is such that I will never cope with it, and an army like me will be needed."

Beneath acres of pumice, secrets aplenty lie awaiting exposure at Akrotiri—frescoes, perhaps in the thousands, opening up new avenues of interpretation, personal treasures too bulky for the owners to have dropped in flight or carted away. There may be a palace with elaborate rooms to shed light on how Akrotiri was governed. And a cemetery, its biological and ritual remains making it a likely repository of significant artifacts, may yet be found. Beyond a small inscription on a pot, no writing has so far turned up; perhaps a deposit of clay tablets awaits a modern decipherer. Then, too, no one can be certain that every Theran left the island in time. It may be that, huddled together near the ancient harbor, are the skeletons of frantic individuals, still clutching their most valuable possessions—people who missed the last boat.

# AN ETERNAL SPRING

More than 1,600 years before the Roman city of Pompeii disappeared under Vesuvius' outpourings, Thera—the Pompeii of the Aegean—perished in a volcanic cataclysm of its own; and as in the case of Pompeii, the very debris that covered the island also suspended it in time, protecting it from the ravages of the ensuing 3,500 years.

Preserved over the eons by ash and pumice, wall paintings unearthed from the site of Akrotiri, on the southern coast of Thera, known later as Santorini, reveal an astonishingly sophisticated culture. No portraits and but one still life adorn the walls of ancient Akrotiri's buildings. Rather, flora and fauna abound in vibrant hues *(above)*, along with human figures intermingling in scenes replete with movement and drama. Most paintings tell a story, and many are so elaborate they defy interpretation. Moreover, the cosmopolitan Therans used imagery from not only nearby Crete and Greece but also more distant lands, such as Egypt.

Like the Romans, Theran artists rendered their ideas directly onto a plaster surface, rubbed to smoothness with pebbles. Although they sketched images over the area before directly applying pigments, painters continuously revised the details, perfecting, for example, a feature of anatomy or the windblown attitude of a flower. Their palettes included reds, yellows, oranges, and browns—all prepared from ochers—black from carbon and manganese, a blue from the mineral glaucophane, and white. Most spectacular, though, was Egyptian blue, an import that was expensive and difficult to obtain.

Most of the works have required some measure of reconstruction, in part because of flaking or crumbling or damage caused by the eruption itself. But by painstakingly piecing together the fragments, archaeologists and restorers have brought back to vivid life many of the ancient masterpieces, several of which appear on the following pages.

The largest intact painting found in any ancient Aegean ruins, the so-called Spring Fresco spreads over 16 square yards along three walls of a ground-floor room in the Delta building at Akrotiri. Lilies in all stages of bloom, appearing to sway in a light breeze, sprout from a landscape of volcanic rocks, while swallows flutter above the buds and blossoms.

Across two walls of Room 6 in the Beta building, vibrant blue monkeys—some of them apparent orchard thieves—scamper up a barren landscape. These nimble primates, which today are found only in Africa, frolic here with enough authenticity to suggest that the artist visited their habitat—or that the creatures were imported to the Cyclades, the group of islands to which Thera belongs.

Beneath a leafy frieze—a standard Minoan motif—two youths spar with each other, while around the corner a pair of antelopes—Oryx beisa, *found only in eastern Africa today*—engage in what may be anything from combat to amorous play. The boxers, which were reconstructed from thousands of plaster fragments, some only a fraction of an inch across, wear belted loincloths under their boyish bellies and gloves on their right hands—the earliest known depiction of this sporting apparel. Their blue heads, believed to indicate the shadow of partially shaved scalps, denote their status as adolescents.

With rouged cheeks and lips, robes with open bodices, and swirling skirts, two female figures under a frieze of stars model what may have been typical Aegean ceremonial fashions. Together with a third (not shown), these images moved their discoverers to name the building in which they appear the House of the Ladies.

From the West House, this fresco of a naked youth holding up his catch—two bundles of mackerel—has survived the millennia remarkably intact. As in the painting of the boxing boys in the Beta building, his shaved scalp shows the stubble of new growth around long locks.

Two ships, part of a fleet included in a 16-inch-high, 20-foot-long fresco that spanned a wall of the West House, glide into a harbor that may be Akrotiri's own. In this section, the populace has turned out in welcome. The fresco may have been done for a wealthy marine Theran official or for a religious house. Some scholars think that the painting records a ceremony or festival whose religious meaning has been lost.

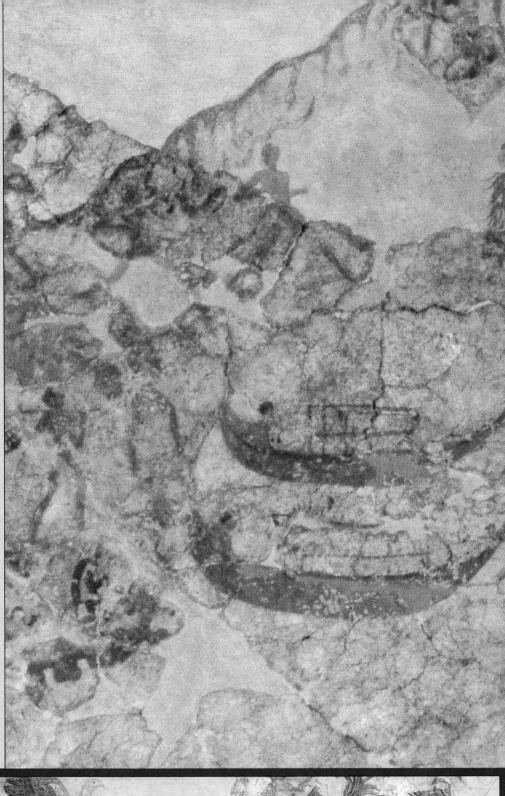

Undulating along the eastern wall of Room 5 of the West House, a vibrantly blue stream bisects a windy subtropical landscape. Although the river is not on a scale to compare with the Nile, the surrounding palms, papyrus, and geese evoke scenes from Egyptian paintings. Panthers and even a flying griffin further enhance the vitality of the colorful work.

# CRETE
# A HUNDRED
# CITIES
# STRONG

For 16 years, the Greek archaeologists Jannis and Efi Sakellarakis, a husband-and-wife team, had been uncovering Minoan remains in northern Crete. Searching a hillside for undiscovered ruins early in the summer of 1979, they came across what might have seemed, to the untrained eye, merely a chunk of carved limestone. The Sakellarakises, however, wondered whether the fragment might have broken off from a type of Minoan sculpture known as "horns of consecration," emblematic bulls' horns that, like the cross or crescent of later religions, sometimes indicated a sacred place. Finding also some Minoan potsherds, the couple decided to excavate the mound. Still, nothing in the tranquil rural setting suggested that what lay beneath would challenge some of the most cherished assumptions of Aegean archaeology.

The hill, on the north slope of Mount Juktas, was known to the local villagers as Anemospilia, "the caves of the wind," because tradition holds that the hollows in its rocks were carved by winter gales blowing off the Aegean. The herb-scented crest lies four miles south of Knossos, celebrated by Homer as the richest of Crete's cities and unearthed by Sir Arthur Evans in the early 1900s.

Above Anemospilia rises the isolated mass of Mount Juktas, its shape, from the north, suggesting a giant's head. In post-Minoan times, Cretans sometimes imagined the gargantuan profile as that of

*Crafted in the image of a bull—a Minoan symbol of strength and fertility—this libation vessel of black steatite, shell, and crystal may have held the blood of sacrificial animals during rituals.*

the classical Greek deity Zeus. A myth told how this sky god, in the guise of a white bull, carried to Crete a Phoenician princess bearing the significant name of Europa. From the union of Zeus and Europa came three sons, including Minos, ruler of Knossos. Whatever fantasy lay at the core of the story, Knossos itself had been real—and every bit as remarkable as portrayed. Here was a glittering palace complex, center of a civilization whose urban comforts rivaled the metropolitan lifestyle of ancient Egypt and was well in advance of those in the rest of Europe.

In the *Iliad,* Homer had sung of "Crete, a hundred cities strong," and indeed, since Evans focused archaeological attention on the spacious Aegean island, hundreds of settlements, many of them Minoan, have been located, including three palaces in addition to Knossos—Phaistos, Mallia, and Zakros—and a number of lesser, but substantial, villas. Yet despite all the marvelous structures and artifacts that have come to light in the process, the Minoans themselves remain hard to pin down. Clearly, they were a major sea power, and their art shows that they lived in close harmony with nature. The archaeological evidence has long been interpreted as reflecting a peaceful, pleasure-loving people living communally with one another and cooperatively with the rest of the world in a kind of Bronze Age utopia. But recent finds—including the Sakellarakises'—hint of a darker side to Minoan life.

It was in the hope of unlocking more of the Minoans' secrets that the Sakellarakises extended their explorations of the hill where they had stumbled upon the piece of limestone. Buoyed by the possibility of unearthing a building of religious significance, the archaeologists assembled a team of University of Athens students and villagers from a nearby town and began digging.

By the end of the first day's excavation, the Sakellarakises had found traces of a walled structure they identified as a sacred enclosure. Though much damaged by some sort of catastrophe, it seemed to consist of three narrow rooms—a central room flanked by two side chambers where, the archaeologists speculated, offerings might have been prepared before being carried to an altar in the central compartment. Access to each chamber was provided by a common corridor, and it was to this space that the archaeologists devoted their initial labors. (Other archaeologists examining the evidence later have suggested that there may also have been three rooms on the other side of the corridor.)

*Greek archaeologist Efi Sakellarakis holds the skull of one of four ancient Cretans she discovered with her husband, Jannis, at Anemospilia in 1979—a find that spawned their controversial conclusion that the Minoans practiced human sacrifice. Pictured above with Efi is Dr. Alexandros Contopoulos, an anthropologist, who helped the Sakellarakises' team examine the skeletons.*

*The more than 400 pottery vessels recovered from a sacred enclosure at Anemospilia allowed archaeologist Jannis Sakellarakis, here inspecting a small clay cup, and his team to speculate about some of the religious activities that may have taken place within its confines.*

At some time in the past, treasure hunters had tried to hack their way into the collapsed and burned building. To their relief, however, the Sakellarakises found the contents of the corridor charred by the fire but not ransacked. Rows of pottery vessels had stood here, probably filled with such offerings as fruit, grain, milk, honey, and wine. While most of the vessels had been smashed, some remained miraculously unbroken and still contained charred fruit seeds.

Examination of the pottery—which proved to be of a specific, datable type, often characterized by floral themes executed in broad brushstrokes of light paint on a dark background—suggested that the shrine at Anemospilia had been built about 1700 BC and was probably in use only about 150 years. The large, carefully hewn blocks of the building, as well as the jars, had fallen at an incline, indicating that the shrine had been rocked and toppled by some natural force, probably an earthquake. There was also evidence that the shrine had been abandoned after its destruction; no pottery of a later period turned up at the site.

Support for the surmise that the place had been destroyed by a cataclysmic event came when the team discovered a crushed skeleton of indeterminate sex in the corridor, the first Minoan human remains to have turned up outside a burial chamber. With renewed vigor, the archaeologists began excavating the central room, wondering whether it contained clues to the shrine's deity. Traces of male and female idols have been found at sacred places on Crete. Minoan images, on frescoes, seals, and ivory statuettes, generally show such icons attired in rich gowns and headdresses. But while wooden effigies must have existed, only hair and extremities, made of stone or bronze, have been found.

As luck would have it, the Sakellarakises did come across evidence of an idol when they went on to dig in the central chamber. There they unearthed fragments of charred wood and a pair of large clay feet with ankles squared off like dowels that might have fitted into a long-skirted wooden torso. The size of the feet suggested a

*All that remains of what the Sakellara-kises believe may have been a statue of a Minoan deity is this pair of life-size clay feet from Anemospilia. Part of a so-called acrolithic idol, these extremities were apparently fashioned from a material different from that used to form the main body—which long ago disintegrated. Because no life-size figures have ever been recovered from any Minoan site, the find is particularly unusual.*

life-size statue, which probably had stood on a raised stone platform, rather like a bench, that occupied the rear wall and had been carved from the hillside. At one end the rock was unhewn, its natural state symbolizing, perhaps, the sacred earth. Shattered pottery remains covered the chamber's entire floor. Exploring further, the archaeologists found, in the room to the east, ceramic vases placed before a ruined stepped altar. These jars were intended for offerings of fruits and liquids, and the central vessel bore, on its rim, an inscription in the early—and as yet undeciphered—Minoan writing known as Linear A *(page 122)*. Then, turning its attention to the west room, the team put in hours of slow, painstaking work through the torpid summer days, with little to show for it.

Excitement revived, however, when three more skeletons were uncovered. Two of them, immediately identifiable as human remains, lay on the floor, and were apparently of persons killed by the earthquake. The third, resting upon a very low altar, was assumed to be the skeleton of a young bull or other sacrificial beast.

While removing the debris from the bones on the altar, a worker exposed a metal object—on the abdomen of the skeleton—that upon closer examination proved to be a bronze weapon, perhaps a knife or spearpoint, 16 inches long and weighing more than a pound. Its keen-edged blade was etched on both sides with the same image—a strange, composite beast with slanted fox's eyes, a boar's snout and tusks, and ears shaped like butterfly wings.

Expecting to identify the remains as those of an animal, Jannis began cleaning the bones. He suddenly tensed. "This was a human being," he announced. "It is hard to believe, but I think we have found a human sacrifice." Aware of the controversy such an interpretation would generate, the archaeologists called upon the forensic expertise of two physical anthropologists at the Athens Medical School Anthropological Museum and an assistant professor of criminology at Athens University. After examining all the evidence, the specialists presented their findings.

The skeleton was that of a male in his late teens, five foot five inches tall, who died lying on his side. His legs were bent so far back that the right heel almost touched the thighbone, suggesting that he might have been trussed like a bull prepared as an offering. The conclusion seemed inescapable to the Sakellarakises and the experts: The young man had indeed been a victim of sacrifice. His throat had been slit, his blood was drained, and then the earthquake struck.

Perhaps the victim had been drugged, one of the experts suggested. Others thought, however, that he might have gone willingly to his death to propitiate the gods, whose rumblings of discontent—as manifested by the tremors—must have been rocking the sanctuary even as the ritual proceeded.

But who in the shrine had wielded the knife? The skeleton farthest from the altar was that of a female aged about 28, who had fallen on her stomach. Although women played an important part in Minoan religious ritual, this one had to be ruled out as a participant for lack of any connecting evidence. The skeleton lying closest to the altar was a more likely suspect. It belonged to a six-foot-tall man in his late thirties, and he wore two ornaments that offered clues to his calling. On the little finger of his left hand was a ring of silver and iron, typical of those found in royal tombs of a later date. The iron covered the silver since it was the rarer and more precious metal of the day, having been usually obtained from meteorites and available only to persons of wealth and high status. Also indicating his importance was a stone seal found near his wrist; it depicted a man in a small boat using a long pole to advance the vessel.

The Sakellarakises referred to the woman and the tall man as priestess and priest. Their deaths were attributed to blows from rocks dislodged from the roof during the earthquake and to the fire that occurred when the oil lamps—also found amid the shrine's rubble—were knocked over.

*Considered by the Sakellarakises to be the vestiges of a ritual sacrifice, this skeleton of a young man—who was about 18 years old at the time of his death—was found on an altar. The couple concluded, from the body's position, that the victim had been trussed in the manner of a sacrificial animal, with his heel bent backward to his thigh. They also suggested that the bronze blade lying on the bones, etched with the image of a strange hybrid animal, inflicted the wound from which the youth's blood flowed.*

The archaeologists and their colleagues now took a closer look at the skeleton that had been found in the corridor. The crushed bones revealed nothing about the man's role in the sacrifice, but the 105 potsherds that lay next to him had much to say. When pieced together they yielded a beautiful piece of pottery, decorated with a red-spotted bull in relief and shaped like a spouted bucket, that could have been used for pouring libations. The Sakellarakises, however, concluded that the vessel had been used to collect the blood of sacrificed bulls. On this occasion, they believed, it had held the blood of the young man.

The archaeologists constructed a scenario of the events that occurred in the Anemospilia shrine on that fateful day more than 3,500 years ago: As earthquakes shook the island, a chief priest, attended by two functionaries, made a desperate attempt to avert disaster by offering up a human sacrifice—possibly his own son. After cutting the victim's throat, the priest laid down the knife and collected the streaming blood. A second priest picked up the blood libation in the spouted bucket used for animal sacrifice, intending to offer it to the idol in the central room. He had only reached the corridor, however, when a violent jolt brought the structure crashing down, entombing all three participants with the youthful sacrifice.

As the Sakellarakises had expected, their theory provoked an uproar that led to a public debate before a packed audience in Athens in 1980. Their fellow Greeks, in particular, were reluctant to believe that their Aegean forebears could have practiced such rites. Many

*From a tomb in southern Crete, this stone sarcophagus covered with plaster and painted in the style of the Minoan frescoes (top) illustrates the ritual slaughter of a bull. While an attendant plays the flute and another places a basket of fruit on an altar, the animal bleeds from the neck into a vessel that resembles the vase (above) discovered at Anemospilia. Standing some two feet high, the vessel, which has been reconstructed, bears the image of a red-spotted bull.*

archaeologists also seemed loath to accept the findings, which contradicted the generally held view of the Minoans as a gentle people.

Some in the academic community accused the Sakellarakises of sensationalism and suggested that the evidence did not warrant the conclusions drawn. Yet hardly had the furor over the Anemospilia discoveries subsided than the British Minoan expert Peter Warren produced more damning evidence of ritual killing as part of Minoan sacrificial tradition. While excavating to the northwest of the palace of Knossos, Warren's team from the British School at Athens found human bones scattered in a basement room of an elegant Late Minoan building that, Warren believed, had been leveled by an earthquake around 1450 BC. Piecing together the 304 bone fragments, experts concluded that they were from two healthy children aged approximately eight and 11.

Twenty-seven of the bones bore knife marks. These were not the crude scars typical of a murderous assault with a bladed weapon; rather, fine grooves suggested that whoever had wielded the knife had used it in a deliberate way after the children were dead. Indeed, the youngsters had probably had their throats cut like the sheep whose bones, bearing similar telltale marks, were found with theirs. Many of the knife marks occurred well away from the joints, indicating that a slicing motion had been used to remove the flesh.

Further evidence that the children had not been the victims of an ordinary murder became apparent when some 37 pottery vessels from the building were examined. Some of these had been stored in four large jars, or pithoi, placed in a first-floor room that had collapsed into the basement as the structure burned. Two of the pithoi contained rhytons used for pouring ritual libations, and Warren deduced they were part of a cult set kept in storage for ritual worship. One of the vases was decorated with a creature that suggested the Gorgon of Greek myth, a winged, snake-haired female with wild staring eyes, large nose, and protruding tongue. This image was of particular help in identifying the divinity associated with the building. Could it be the great Minoan goddess of nature, who was sometimes depicted entwined with snakes? An old theory suggested that the Greek Gorgon has its origins in just such a divinity.

A second grisly aspect of the goddess's worship at this time and place was brought to light in a room close to the chamber where the youngsters' remains were discovered. Here the archaeologists found a vessel containing shells, children's finger bones, and a vertebra bearing the mark of a knife—remnants perhaps of a meal—as well as burned earth. While the contents may have been symbolic offerings to the nature goddess, Peter Warren thinks it possible that the flesh was actually consumed by her human worshipers, after the goddess had been invoked by ecstatic dancing.

His surmise is based in part on a classical Greek myth, possibly Cretan in origin, relating how a mythical being named Zagreus was lured by the Titans, torn to pieces and devoured, then brought to life again. Zagreus was linked, in classical times, to Zeus Kretagenes, a youthful fertility god of Crete, who was killed and resurrected through rituals involving his consort, the nature goddess. This god is also linked by some to Dionysus, of whom the same tale is told. (Coincidentally, the Egyptian god Osiris suffered a similar fate and was also resurrected.) By eating human flesh, Warren argued, Minoans may have identified themselves with the reborn god, and thus with the earth-goddess, source of fertility.

The possibility that Minoans engaged in these cannibalistic rites calls to mind the court of King Minos, at Knossos, as it was portrayed in Greek myth. It was said that Poseidon, god of the sea, sent to King Minos a white bull for sacrifice, but that the avaricious Minos kept it. To punish him the god inflicted his queen, Pasiphaë, with a passion for the bull. The cunning craftsman Daedalus, an exile from Athens, arranged to satisfy the queen's lust by making a wooden cow, in which she concealed herself and seduced the bull. The resulting offspring was the monstrous Minotaur, half bull, half man, which Daedalus imprisoned in the Labyrinth, a maze beneath the palace of Knossos, where it fed on youths and maidens sent as tribute to Minos from Athens.

Fantastic as the tale may sound, it contains elements that chime with known facts. Bulls, for example, were important to Minoan ritual. The discovery of the children's bones suggests cannibalism, enhancing further the notion held by some scholars that Greek myths often embody ancient, if distorted, memories of real practices and events. Other archaeologists have argued that myths are far too unreliable to be used as historical documentation or compared with archaeological findings. And one scholar has mused that the children's bones may be the residue from some Minoan serial killer's nefarious activities.

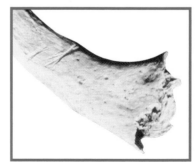

Yet Warren's physical evidence of sacrifice is considered persuasive by many archaeologists who have pondered the circumstanc-

*Chilling evidence of the possible sacrifice of children came to light at Knossos when archaeologist Peter Warren, excavating what came to be called the Room of the Children's Bones* (above), *discovered the telltale remains of a rib, a right femur, and a clavicle* (left, top to bottom). *The knife marks they bear indicate that the flesh was stripped from the bones in a manner used for sacrificed animals. Piecing together 23 bone fragments to form a pair of skulls* (inset, top), *Warren's team used such evidence to confirm that the two victims were ages eight and 11.*

es. Since the building was apparently destroyed around the same time the children were killed, some have speculated that, as at Anemospilia, their sacrifice had been designed to avert disaster. But to Warren, it seems an inappropriate act—removing and eating human flesh in the hope of averting a natural calamity. The inference, he insists, must be that child sacrifice and ritual cannibalism were an established part of Minoan religious practice. This conclusion, as Warren acknowledges, "constitutes a rather startling challenge" to the traditional image of the Minoans "as one of the gentler of the world's ancient cultures."

The early notion of Minoans as serene and peaceful was based in part on the observations by Evans and other archaeologists that Minoan towns were built on flat ground near the sea and that their palaces appeared to be unfortified. Since this seemingly left them vulnerable to attack, the assumption was that they in fact did not need to be defended either from an outside enemy or from one another. This once-accepted opinion has been further challenged by several archaeologists who have found what they believe to be military elements in Early and Middle Minoan Crete, including fortified sites that may have functioned as watchtowers, and structures that may possibly be defensive walls at some of the palace sites. The city of Mallia, for one, was surrounded by a wall of mud brick, built on stone foundations that still can be seen.

Traditionally, scholars have been content to think that a fleet of warships protected Crete, as ancient Greek historians believed. Others suggest that the island's isolation, far from the Levantine and Egyptian coasts, prevented maritime aggression from Near Eastern states. Only inhabitants of the Aegean area could have mounted the necessary naval expedition, although for centuries they probably had neither the strength nor the unity required for the endeavor.

Nevertheless, by Late Minoan times, the Cretans possessed all the contemporary weapons of organized warfare—daggers, swords, rapiers, axes, and javelins. But these may have been kept simply as symbols of power within the community or used in policing the island. The chief personal article of defense seems to have been a full-length shield, sometimes rectangular or sometimes shaped like a figure eight, and made of bull's hide stretched over a wooden frame. Helmets, too, were worn, not only for quasi-military activities but also to protect the heads of contestants in boxing bouts. Some scholars suggest that boxing and other popular Minoan athletic activities may have served as a form of paramilitary training.

Wary of overstating their case, the Sakellarakises have taken pains to insist that, in their view, the sacrifice at Anemospilia was an unprecedented event, born of desperation in the face of a terrible disaster. Their caution is justified by the artistic record, which, with few exceptions, is free of the violent themes—war, punishment of wrongdoers, abasement of inferiors—which recur in the art of the Bronze Age Egyptians and Babylonians.

Unless military imagery was rejected out of aesthetic sensitivity, it is easy, and perhaps valid, to draw the conclusion, as many have done, that the Minoans were indeed placid, enjoying lives so blithe and sunny that they appear to a few modern eyes as decadent and enervated. Some think that Homer had in mind the Cretans when, in the *Odyssey,* he drew a picture of the mythical Phaeacians. "Speedy runners, and the best of seamen," they confessed that "dear to us ever is the banquet, and the harp, and the dance, and changes of raiment, and the warm bath, and love, and sleep."

Comfortable living in surroundings of grace and charm is the hallmark of the Minoan palaces and villas. The communal rooms of the palaces were often decorated with alabaster veneering, and their plaster walls were painted with scenes from nature or court ceremonies. Domestic accommodations were typically spacious and commodious, yet the style and proportions of the rooms are usually on a human scale. Such quarters had areas that have been interpreted as bathrooms, with elaborate drainage systems; and, as diggings have shown, there was at least one toilet at Knossos. Light wells and interior courts ensured adequate illumination and ventilation. Columned porticoes allowed the residents to step out onto private, enclosed terraces.

Special circumstances may have prevailed on Crete, encouraging the Minoans to live in basic harmony with one another. The isolated position of Crete in the Early Bronze Age probably produced an unusually homogeneous population. The resulting uniformity of customs and speech no doubt stimulated sharing and cooperation, perhaps obviating—initially, at least—the need for a strong, central authority. In such an atmosphere of goodwill the first palaces took shape, around 1900 BC; actually, they seem more like community

# THE ART OF BULL LEAPING: A CURIOUS AND DANGEROUS SPECTACLE

Performing death-defying feats of gymnastic prowess before crowds of eager spectators, young male and female Cretans pitted their agility and courage in competition against bulls, bursting with vigor and menace, in what may have been ancient Crete's favorite sport: bull leaping. Enacting a sort of acrobatic dance around the bull, these daring men and women—probably teenagers—apparently attempted a variety of perilous flips and vaults through the animal's horns and over its back—movements that have been judged potentially fatal, if not impossible, by modern bullfighters and rodeo riders.

Minoan art and sculpture is rich with scenes of bull leaping, portraying dark- and light-skinned figures—representing male and female—singly or in teams, capturing bulls in the wild *(below)* and executing astonishing maneuvers *(overleaf)*. However, until Linear A, the written language of the Minoan civilization, is deciphered, the significance of bull leaping will remain an enigma.

It is likely that the events took place at major festivals—perhaps those in the spring that celebrated fertility and rebirth. But whether the activity was merely an exciting and spectacular—though dangerous—sport using skilled athletes or, perhaps, a ritual that evolved from the capture of wild bulls for religious sacrifice is not known.

What does seem clear, though, is that the animals suffered no harm, as they do in modern Spanish bullfighting, although they were probably sacrificed after the event. Even the risk to the athletes may not have been as great as it appears, for archaeologists have discovered caches of bull horns with their sharp points filed down to bluntness.

*This cup of gold illustrates in repoussé what may be an attempt to trap wild bulls for sporting events on Crete. The 3½-inch-wide surface, seen here in a rollout, shows one bull trampling a man as a second figure—a young girl, according to Sir Arthur Evans—grasps the animal's horns. Another bull is caught in a rope net, while a third escapes behind a palm tree.*

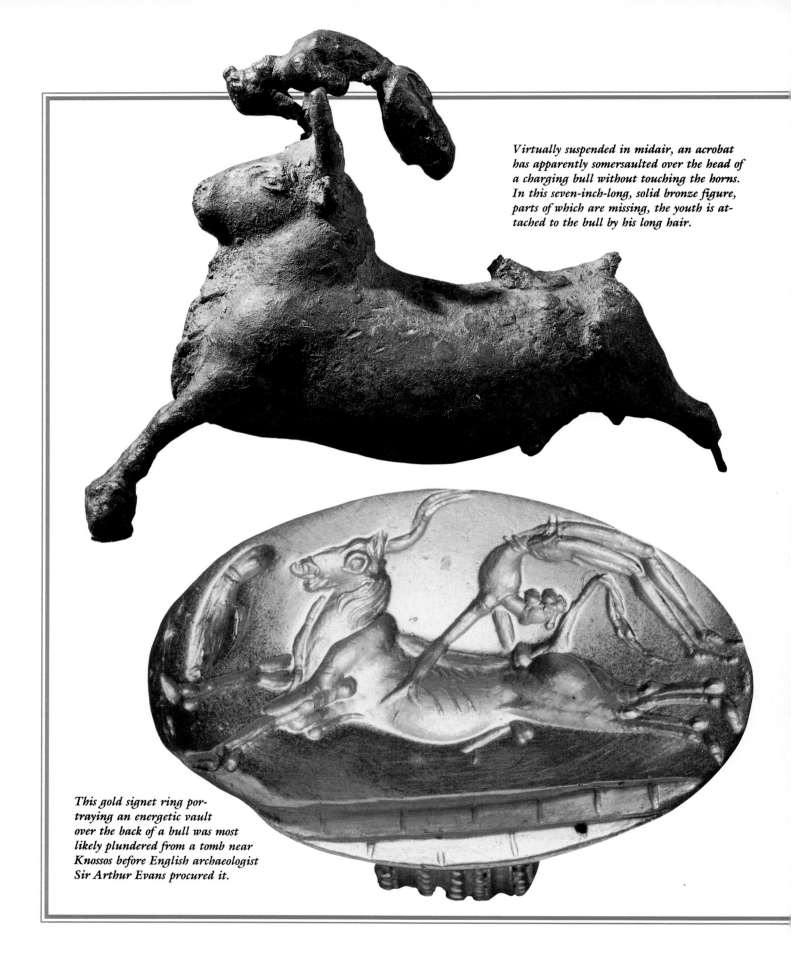

Virtually suspended in midair, an acrobat has apparently somersaulted over the head of a charging bull without touching the horns. In this seven-inch-long, solid bronze figure, parts of which are missing, the youth is attached to the bull by his long hair.

This gold signet ring portraying an energetic vault over the back of a bull was most likely plundered from a tomb near Knossos before English archaeologist Sir Arthur Evans procured it.

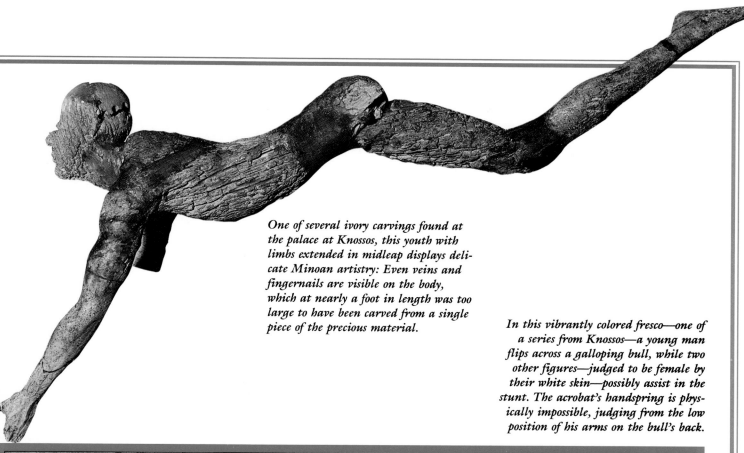

One of several ivory carvings found at the palace at Knossos, this youth with limbs extended in midleap displays delicate Minoan artistry: Even veins and fingernails are visible on the body, which at nearly a foot in length was too large to have been carved from a single piece of the precious material.

In this vibrantly colored fresco—one of a series from Knossos—a young man flips across a galloping bull, while two other figures—judged to be female by their white skin—possibly assist in the stunt. The acrobat's handspring is physically impossible, judging from the low position of his arms on the bull's back.

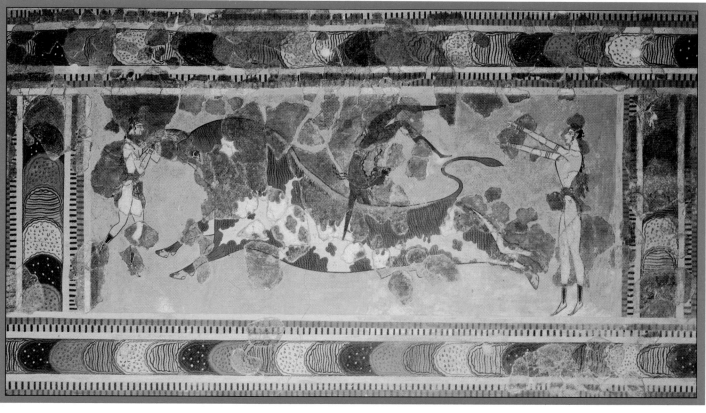

centers—with workrooms, storerooms, markets, housing, and religious facilities—than the residences of monarchs.

Not only was Cretan society ethnically homogeneous, but, especially in the early phase of Minoan development, it also, according to many scholars, seems to have been relatively egalitarian, although there must have been leaders of some kind. As a grave often reflects its occupant's status in life, so burial patterns in a culture provide clues to social stratification. Tombs from the earliest Minoan era, beginning around the middle of the third millennium BC, are generally large, round structures five to 14 yards in diameter, possibly with flat wattle-and-daub roofs. The numerous skeletons in each tomb have led some archaeologists to suggest that many of these enclosures contain the remains of a single family group, a lineage buried over generations, indicative of a people organized by kinship in small egalitarian villages. Such a community was Myrtos; between 2600 and 2200 BC, it was the site of a small hamlet of stone and mud-brick buildings, covering no more than 1,500 square yards.

Gradually, during this early formative phase of Minoan civilization, the people lost some of their personal and local autonomy as larger regional centers evolved, some of which became the first palaces. Society grew more hierarchical in this era, known as the Old Palace Period, which began around 1900 BC and lasted until about 1700 BC, when, it is believed, an earthquake shook Crete and flattened the first of these structures. All were rebuilt, and a new one took shape on the east coast of Zakros. Minoan palace culture reached its zenith in the next two centuries, from 1700 to 1470 BC, an epoch archaeologists refer to as the New Palace Period.

In the evolving social structure of the island, the palace personnel were probably at the top. Secondary centers known as villas were built throughout the territories controlled by the palaces, and these managed the goods that flowed from the countryside to the palaces and back again. Because of their importance, villa administrators must have been at the next level, with townspeople and farmers at the bottom. As an indicator of the growing importance attached to personal wealth and status, single burials took place with greater frequency. Still, the continuing practice of communal interment suggests that class distinctions remained somewhat blurred. Archaeologists reason that there probably existed a unified social structure based on kinship or nonfamily groups, membership in

*Dubbed La Parisienne for her rouged lips, the beguiling woman pictured in this fresco fragment from the palace at Knossos is probably a robed priestess or even a goddess. The sacral knot at the back of her neck—which seems to have been part of a ceremonial costume—may indicate her role in a religious function.*

*Considered one of the great Minoan masterpieces, this 16-inch-high ivory figure wearing gold sandals was reassembled from pieces found in the late 1980s. Some archaeologists suggest that the figure may represent a youthful Zeus and that the god so well known to the classical Greeks could thus have been worshiped hundreds of years earlier on Minoan Crete.*

which perhaps depended on occupation or birth. As social stratification increased, regional authority seems to have become more and more centralized. During this phase, Knossos may have expanded its power base, possibly controlling most of central and northern Crete.

By now, the palaces were hubs of Minoan religious and economic life. Sacred artifacts have been found throughout their premises, with many of the rooms set aside for cult purposes. For the areas of the island under their sway, they were centers for the production of goods, the storage of food, raw materials, and finished articles, and for the dispersion of these items through foreign trade. Farmers brought their surpluses to the villas and palaces, where the products would be held or processed for use in paying for imports, to compensate palace administrative personnel or other workers, or for distribution among Minoans who could not produce their own food. Whether the peasants brought their output to the palaces in response to a tax or levy, or as payment in kind for their land is not known; nor is it understood exactly how the Minoans distributed the vessels, tools, jewelry, clothing, ritual items, and other articles they had manufactured in the warren of palace workshops or had imported from abroad. Since records of all these economic activities were kept in Linear A, a script that has yet to be translated and of which only a few fragments survive, there is no documentation to guide the archaeologists.

The question of who ruled Minoan Crete in its heyday is another puzzler. Minos, the name of the legendary king of Knossos, may have been a title, like pharaoh. But Minos may not have been the single absolute ruler of the island. Some researchers have looked to the Greek myths for guidance. Traditionally, the three sons of Zeus and Europa—Minos, Rhadamanthys, and Sarpedon—are associated, respectively, with the palaces of Knossos, Phaistos, and Mallia. Perhaps their kinship—providing this was the case—made for a friendly balance of power. If myth is any clue to reality, the legendary brothers were good kings, for the Greeks posthumously rewarded Minos and Rhadamanthys for their just rules by making them judges in the Greek afterworld.

Although the layout and appointments of the Minoan palaces imply that they were occupied by kings and queens, some scholars note that images of rulers do not dominate Minoan art, as they do that of the Minoans' Egyptian contemporaries. Yet other archaeologists argue that a better understanding of the figures portrayed in Minoan art might lead to the opposite conclusion. Evans, for example, thought he could identify portraits of a king and a prince in seal impressions from Knossos, but since the accompanying symbols have not been deciphered, no one can say for certain what titles or powers these individuals actually possessed. Nevertheless, Evans concluded that supreme authority probably was wielded by a dynasty of priest-kings ruling in the name of the supreme deity—the nature goddess—rather than as absolute monarchs in their own right, a notion that has since been discarded.

Because so many palace rooms seem to have been reserved for rituals, some students of the Minoans think that the administration was essentially theocratic. Indeed, one scholar has suggested that the Minoan palaces could only have been built by the voluntary participation of the entire population, laboring not out of fear of a tyrant's lash but in the belief that they were constructing a home for the goddess, in which the king would live as her representative.

Whatever the source of their power, the Minoan rulers may have been kept in check by a large consultative body—a council of elders or of the nobility, including landed gentry stationed at the villas, or even a popular assembly drawn from all levels of society. Some students of the culture believe that it was to accommodate such assemblies that large courtyards, called theatral areas, were built outside the palaces. Here the royalty, attended by their retinue, would appear to the multitude, walking ceremonially to these areas along paved processional pathways leading from the palace entrances.

The leaders, whoever they were, may have been responsible for the picture of serenity that seems to pervade Minoan frescoes and other artistic remains. One view, gaining ground among the rising generation of archaeologists, is that the pastoral and nautical imagery was deliberately created to reinforce the notion of a highly unified, satisfied society; in other words, that it was propaganda to reinforce the view of the ruling class as benefactors.

The apparent unity of religious belief in Minoan society may mask contradictions. Although the goddess of fertility and agricultural renewal is most often viewed as being the Minoans' su-

*Fantastic beasts, like the one seen here only faintly on the bottom of this stone triton from Mallia, adorn some of the finest art objects recovered from ancient Crete and Greece. Some archaeologists think such figures may be deities linked to the Egyptian hippopotamus goddess, Tawaret. Crescent shapes incised over the entire surface imitate actual shells.*

Lovers of nature, Minoan artists celebrated their world in a range of media, as is shown by this sampling of creations: a mural from the House of the Frescoes at Knossos depicting a bluebird surrounded by flowering plants (left); from Zakros, a delicate butterfly carved from imported ivory that fire has turned gray (above); and from Phaistos, an elegant pottery jug covered with a grass pattern.

preme divinity, it is also possible that she may have been their only one, and that the other deities were merely representations of her various attributes. There is little evidence of a male god, although classical Greek myths, such as those of Zeus Kretagenes or Dionysus, have led to speculations concerning the death and resurrection of a young god of vegetation. One myth tells how Minos' son Glaucos, who was drowned in a jar of honey (used in the ancient world for embalming), was restored to life with an herb revealed by a snake.

Greek myths also place the birth of Zeus, ruler of the gods, on Crete. In mythology, Mother Earth took Zeus' pregnant mother, Rhea, to Crete to have her child, there to hide him from his voracious father, Cronus. Warned that one of his children would supersede him, Cronus was in the habit of eating his offspring. When Zeus grew strong enough, he defeated Cronus, forcing him to regurgitate his swallowed progeny. But archaeologists naturally prefer to rely on concrete discoveries, such as the goddess represented in exquisite faience figures from Knossos, entwined with snakes and dressed in characteristic Late Minoan mode, with heavy flounced skirt and apron and fitted, tight-waisted jacket that exposes her full breasts. Although usually taken as a goddess, this female figure is sometimes shown participating in ceremonies as a priestess.

While the palaces seem to have fulfilled religious functions, worship was not confined to these grand structures. Nothing that could be considered a temple has ever been dug up on Crete, although small sacred enclosures have been found, such as the one at Anemospilia uncovered by the Sakellarakises. Since the Minoan religion focused on a nature goddess, a great deal of ritual associated with her took place in the countryside around specially designated trees or groves, in caves, or atop hallowed peaks. One fresco, among many art objects that illustrate this point, has been called *The Sacred Grove* by archaeologists and shows a grove of olive trees where men perform a ceremony in which women dance.

If a goddess or goddesses were central to Minoan religious life, it is likely that women had important cult status in Minoan society. Indeed, priestesses are widely portrayed in the art. Most archaeologists today believe that a stone seat found in the Throne Room at Knossos was not, as Evans believed, the throne of Minos, but of a priestess-queen. This is based on the notion that the room resembles a central shrine, where women would have participated in rites to the female deity. Indeed, some students of Minoan culture

## AN EARTHLY FORM OF WORSHIP

In the eyes of the Minoans, spirit pervaded the natural world—a belief that led them to transmute any number of outdoor settings into sanctuaries for worshiping their pantheon. Caves, for example, offered a solemn opportunity to commune with various gods and the powers of darkness. Some 30 rock niches on Crete have yielded innumerable clay offerings—evidence of religious practices—in their damp, uninhabitable recesses, and several of the more impressive caverns contained gold double axes, bronze figurines, and the remnants of animal sacrifices.

Many mountain summits, situated away from the bustle of palaces and villages, are littered with terra-cotta votive offerings. While these include a few human figures in the attitude of worship, most consist of small, crude animal shapes such as cattle and sheep. The presence on peak sanctuaries of clay models of limbs suggests that the offerings may have been intended for a healing deity. The Minoans appear to have lighted great bonfires—probably at nightfall—on these sky-high sanctuaries and tossed their gifts into the blaze.

Judging from the iconography in their frescoes, jewelry, and other art, the Minoans created sacred havens in the open country as well, at sites of trees such as crop-bearing olives and figs, which were crucial to their well-being and the economy.

Mentioned in the Odyssey, *this hillside cavern named for Ei-leithyia*—in mythology a nymph who protected women in childbirth—*drew worshipers from Stone Age times to Roman, as was revealed by potsherds on the cave's floor. Although no proof exists that the Minoans worshiped a fertility deity here, the stalagmites visible in the photo may have been seen as natural images of a mother goddess and her child.*

Found in a grave at Archanes, this gold signet ring—which probably dates to the Mycenaean occupation of Crete—shows the importance of the tree in Minoan worship. Leaves sweep over the heads of a female figure—who may be a goddess or a priestess—and two men in attitudes of rapture.

This votive bronze of a Minoan man performing a traditional gesture of worship is unusual because the figure is heavyset rather than thin-waisted, as is the young male typically depicted in Minoan art.

A goat climbs the face of a mountain in this detail (far right) *from a 12-inch-high rhyton* (right), *found in the palace at Zakros, that illustrates the sacred embellishments of a peak sanctuary set in the wilderness. Carved in low relief over the entire surface of the stone vessel—once enhanced with gold leaf—the scene depicts a mountain rising from a sparse, rocky landscape, at the summit of which is an enclosed triple shrine containing several altars for various ceremonies. Wild goats sitting on top of the roof and birds in flight complete the picture.*

maintain that Crete must have been a theocratic state ruled by priestesses, whose ability to speak for the divine gave them the power to direct the state's actions.

While sticking to the more cautious line that Minoan Crete was ruled by kings, one scholar has suggested that "succession to the throne was through the female line by marriage to the king's daughter." In other respects, too, Minoan society may have been matrilineal, with children named after their mother and all inheritance conferred through the female line. Such customs arise in primitive societies where people do not comprehend a direct connection between a baby and its father. This line of reasoning is based on the tradition that these matrilineal customs survived until the fourth century BC among the Carians and Lycians of Anatolia—peoples who, according to legend, were descended from the Minoans.

Whether or not women actually took part in the day-to-day governance of Crete, they appear vivacious and animated in frescoes, and seem to have enjoyed respect and freedom in everyday life. Women took an active part in the bull-leaping ceremonies—a dubious privilege, perhaps *(pages 91-93)*. Also, as is shown in the so-called Grandstand Fresco, which depicts men and women watching an event, women also formed a sizable proportion of the audience, occupying places of honor or mingling with the men.

Ladies of the Minoan court lavished much attention on their appearance; in the palaces, they had rooms devoted especially to their toilettes, equipped with beauty aids— bronze hand mirrors, wood and ivory combs, jewelry boxes, and cosmetics to enhance the redness

of their lips or the whiteness of their cheeks. The basic female costume was the breast-baring bodice and the long flounced skirt. These garments varied in their features and decorations—sometimes they were patterned with geometrical designs; sometimes they were elaborately covered with animals, possibly rendered in embroidery, as in Egypt. During the later Minoan era, the long skirt often had a marked V in front, and some examples appear to have been divided. Wool cloth was the staple material, but linen—perhaps imported from Egypt—was doubtless available. Dyestuffs derived from minerals and plants were varied and plentiful. Saffron crocuses most likely were cultivated both for making yellow dye and for flavoring food. A charming wall picture from 17th-century BC Knossos shows a pet monkey pulling up saffron flowers. Alluringly attired, women often left a ringlet dangling in front of their ears (as did some men), but generally they wore their hair in much more elaborate coiffures, sometimes piled high on top of the head and held in place with ribbons, diadems, hair nets, and ornamental pins.

A leisured and gracious lifestyle must be paid for, and it is apparent that privileged Minoans had the means to do so. For most of their basic needs—grain and meat, oil and wine, fuel and clothing—the populace was self-sufficient. Today the oak and pine forests that supplied the Minoans with timber are gone, victims of charcoal making and overgrazing, but as recently as the 17th century AD, the island—known as Candia in the medieval and early modern world—was regarded as a fount of plenty. Describing the country around Khania, in the western part of Crete, in 1609, the Scottish traveler William Lithgow wrote: "For

*Discovered in the ruins of a villa, the intricately carved steatite "Harvester's Vase"—seen here in two views—illustrates a lively procession of workers apparently wending their way to or from the fields. Walking in pairs, some of the 27 figures carry rods for winnowing grain and appear to be singing, while one plays an Egyptian instrument known as a sistrum (opposite). The leader of the group—who may be performing priestly duties—wears a fringed robe adorned with a pattern of scales signifying his status (below). The low relief is carved into a band only three inches high.*

beauty, pleasure and profit, it may easily be surnamed the garden of the whole Universe, being the goodliest plot, the Diamond sparke, and the Honny-spot of all Candy." Yet this bountiful land lacked two ingredients essential to a great Bronze Age civilization—the tin and copper necessary to make bronze.

The exact origin of the copper and tin the Minoan metalsmiths used is an unsolved archaeological riddle. Copper sources in the Aegean, on Cyprus, and in Afghanistan are well known; in addition, speculation centers on the mountains of central Europe, Turkey, or possibly even the hills of Cornwall, England. Precious metals had also to be imported. Gold and silver were shipped from Egypt, the Aegean Islands, southeastern Attica, or western Anatolia. The island of Melos, in the Cyclades, provided the black obsidian used for vases and some seals. From the southern Peloponnesus came fine stones for making bowls and other seals, while the emery used in shaping them was shipped from Naxos. Ivory for seals, combs, amulets, and boxes probably reached Crete from Syria. Ostrich eggs, which the Minoans fashioned into libation jars, may have been obtained from northwest Africa or Egypt, which also supplied Crete with alabaster and finished jewelry, such as scarab pendants. The monkeys depicted on frescoes also may have been introduced from Egypt, along with cats. Figurines and finished seals arrived from as far away as Mesopotamia.

Cretan products must have been exchanged for these goods. Minoan painted wares, jewelry, bronze daggers, and vessels of precious metal have been found throughout the eastern Mediterranean. Especially valued was Kamares ware, exquisite pottery manufactured

*Representing Minoan houses, these miniature faience plaques, which once may have adorned a wooden box, illustrate the architectural style of dwellings on ancient Crete. The flat-roofed buildings stand two or three stories tall. Double doors and mullioned windows grace their stone, clay, and timber-framed facades.*

in palace workshops and named after the sacred cave on Mount Ida where it was first found in 1890. Typically in this pottery white, orange, and red loops, diamonds, and circles whirl and twist on a black background. Using very pure clay, master craftsmen could create pots as thin as bone-china teacups.

The bulk of the exports, however, probably consisted of basic materials such as food, cloth, and timber, brought to the palace and stored there prior to shipment. Olive oil, a staple of the region, could have been one of Crete's major commodities; at Knossos, Evans found a storage area containing numerous huge jars meant to hold oil, with a total capacity of more than 60,000 gallons. Other valuable Cretan trade items included perfumes and medicines concocted from local plants, such as mint, sage, and celery.

Underpinning Minoan trade was the Minoan navy. From the Old Palace Period onward, Crete maintained intermittent sea communication with the eastern Mediterranean. Early ships probably either lacked rudders and masts or had, at most, one mast. Since few

*This 9.4-inch-high terra-cotta model provides a rare three-dimensional view of a Minoan villa. An inside staircase leads up to the second level, where columns support a flat roof and a balcony juts out on rounded beams.*

harbors had yet been built, vessels had to be small enough to be drawn up on a beach or moored in shallow water. But by the New Palace Period, depictions on seals and impressions left by them suggest the construction of ships possibly up to 100 feet long, manned by crews of 50 and equipped with multiple sails, rudders, decks, gangways, cabins, and battering rams. Harbors constructed around the coast now offered safe havens to deep-draft vessels and direct sailing routes to all points of the compass. By this time, Cretan goods might have been channeled into overseas markets through trading stations established on foreign soil.

Links between Crete and Egypt seem to have been particularly strong—and not just in terms of commerce. The Egyptians left many records of their apparently cordial dealings with the people they called Keftiu. Official pharaonic records of about 1500 BC mention that the ships of Keftiu transported Palestinian timber to Egypt. A papyrus dating from a century earlier refers to Cretan medicines. And a school slate of the same period includes various Cretan placenames, written as exercises for pupils. At Egypt's Thebes, in the tomb of Rekhmere, vizier to Thutmose III, who reigned between 1504 and 1450 BC, foreigners dressed in non-Egyptian loincloths of the type portrayed on Cretan frescoes and portrayed carrying precious items are described as coming from "the land of Keftiu and of the islands in the middle of the Great Green Sea." This is one of some half-dozen tombs with similar depictions.

Minoan supremacy of the sea was treated as historical fact by the fifth-century BC Greek historian Thucydides, who wrote: "Minos is the earliest of all those known to us by tradition who acquired a navy." Scholars wonder whether the Cretans used their naval power simply to service and protect their trading interests, or whether they exploited it in the spirit of conquest, creating in effect a Minoan empire. Thucydides, who believed it to be a law of nature that men will rule wherever they can, was in no doubt that the Minoans followed expansionist policies. Minos, he recorded, "made himself master of a very great part of what is now called the Hellenic Sea, and became lord of the Cyclades and first colonizer of most of them, driving out the Carians and establishing his own sons in them as governors. Piracy, too, he tried to clear from the sea, as far as he could, desiring that revenues should come to him more readily."

*Intact today, the paved Royal Road at Knossos led to the palace and connected areas outside the confines that were used for processions and ceremonies. The only survivor of the Minoan palaces, Knossos was probably last inhabited by the Mycenaeans, after they took over Crete.*

Pursuing the notion that the Minoans might have been colonizers, archaeologists have found, on some islands such as Kea, Melos, and Thera, groups of houses, no different from the other houses there but with interior furnishings that are distinctively Cretan. Finds of Minoan pottery or fragments of wall paintings also suggest a Minoan presence on Rhodes, Metus, and Cyprus. This evidence represents the strong impact of Crete during the New Palace Period, as Minoan ideas were adapted by the islanders. Also, Minoans may have come to live on these islands to facilitate the trade in raw materials and finished products; indeed, there are indications of such a colony of Cretans on Kythera. Many archaeologists believe that the Cretans controlled a string of trading posts throughout a network of Minoanized Aegean islands.

As if to celebrate their fruitful relationship with the sea, Minoan potters of around 1500 BC developed what is known as the Marine Style, decorating their wares with extraordinarily lifelike octopuses, dolphins, paper nautiluses, shellfish, corals, and sponges, set against naturalistic backgrounds of rock and seaweed. As the fruits of foreign trade made their way back to Crete, opulent new mansions sprang up all over the island. But these were the last brilliant flickers of a flame soon to be extinguished. In the space of no more than a century, the whole intricate edifice of Minoan civilization came crashing down. About 1470 BC, all the great palaces except Knossos were devastated by fire, together with their surrounding towns and all of the villas. At the same time, Minoan trading posts and settlements overseas were abandoned or razed.

Like so many issues surrounding the Minoans, the nature of the destruction is in dispute. Convinced that Minoan domination of the Aegean remained unbroken right to the end, Evans believed that the glory days of Crete were shattered by an earthquake that leveled Knossos, which thereafter became the home of a squatter population. His views, based on pottery sequences at Knossos, were first challenged in the 1930s by archaeologists who, having studied the evidence both on Crete and on the Greek mainland, concluded that in that last century before the fall of Knossos, there had been a struggle between the Minoans and the Mycenaeans, from which the mainlanders emerged victorious and took control of Crete.

This interpretation is now accepted as the correct one. What the archaeological record indicates is that a foreign presence existed on Crete after 1470 BC. Warrior graves and massive caches of weapons contribute to the air of chilly military grandeur that must have pervaded Knossos at this time. Even more tellingly, the Minoan system of writing, Linear A, disappeared, to be replaced by the script called Linear B, the earliest form of written Greek.

Thus the Post-Palace Period, from 1470 to 1380 BC, was controlled by the island's new Mycenaean overlords. Knossos, which had been partly razed in 1470, was the only palace rebuilt, presumably to serve as a center from which the Mycenaeans could dominate the island. Life in the palace continued, and elsewhere on the island are signs of another century of vitality.

How the Mycenaeans actually assumed power is still debated. They may have wrested it from the Minoans by conquest. Perhaps the Minoans were weakened and divided by natural catastrophe such as the earlier eruption on Thera, interdynastic wars, or internal revolt against an increasingly tyrannical and rapacious government. It is widely agreed that even if much of Crete survived the upheaval of 1470, there must have been far-reaching economic, religious, and political repercussions, possibly leading to social unrest or to a lack of trust in the palace system. This would have left Crete easier prey to Mycenaean invaders. On the other hand, since close trading links must have existed between the two cultures, the Mycenaean takeover may have been achieved more peacefully than might be imagined— through intermarriage of members of the ruling families.

The Mycenaean occupation of the palace of Knossos was short-lived, however. In about 1380 BC the edifice was destroyed by fire. Again the precise cause is not known; another earthquake, internal wars, or a wave of invaders have each been suggested. All that can be said with any certainty is that the end came abruptly, without warning, in the spring or summer. This time no new Minoan culture was to rise phoenixlike from the ashes. Eventually, darkness and obscurity descended on the Aegean realms. Its great era over, the once-bustling island awaited another fate: Half a millennium later it would become an outpost of the classical world, its glorious past to be half remembered and perpetuated in Greek myths.

# PALACES AND LABYRINTHS

The mighty King Minos, Greek myth relates, ruled his wealthy maritime kingdom from his huge and sumptuous palace at Knossos. The ruins of the edifice exist, excavated in the early part of the century by Sir Arthur Evans, and verify Minoan power. Unlike palaces on the Greek mainland, those on Crete served not only as royal residences but also as centers of religion, government, craftsmanship, and commerce. Knossos was a labyrinth of bustling workshops and counting houses, bursting storerooms, lavish public precincts, and ornate shrines. In a special throne room, a priestess supplicated the fertility goddess while seated on the finely carved gypsum chair above, called "the oldest throne in Europe" by Evans, who unearthed it in 1900.

Knossos' plan was mimicked in part by the palaces at Phaistos, Zakros, and Mallia, the three other royal edifices thus far excavated on Crete. At the core of each—and of palace life—lay a great open court. Around it,

like the outward-growing rings of a tree, spread rooms of various sizes arranged in several stories. An external court running along the richly ornamented western exterior served as a backdrop for public processions and ceremonies.

This scheme endured throughout the nearly six centuries that Minoan palaces stood. They first appeared around 1900 BC. In about 1700, at the end of what historians call the Old Palace Period, a cataclysm—perhaps an earthquake followed by conflagrations—destroyed them. The rich and dauntless Minoans rebuilt, more grandly than before.

A series of further disasters, again accompanied by fire, possibly as a result of invasion, leveled Phaistos, Zakros, and Mallia once more, ending the New Palace Period around 1470 BC. Knossos alone survived, to be occupied, during a Post-Palace Period lasting until 1380 BC, by a powerful foreign dynasty that likely held sway over the rest of the island.

Commanding a sweeping panorama of the fertile Mesara Valley as well as the sea, Phaistos dominates a prominent ridge on Crete's southern coast. Its plan typifies those of Minoan palaces: Rooms of all sizes cluster around a colonnaded central court. To the west of the building lies a two-part court joined by a broad flight of steps.

**P**haistos, Minoan Crete's second most important city and third largest palace, boasts perhaps its most glorious view, north to 6,000-foot-high Mount Ida. Partway to the summit, visible from the palace's central courtyard, is the sacred Kamares cave, which gave its name to the exquisite pottery that archaeologists found in a great cache there as well as abundantly throughout the royal structures. During the Old Palace Period, workshops turned out large quantities of this vividly multicolored ware. The flowing decorative style that distinguishes Minoan pottery in general took inspiration from the forms of nature, as in the superb flowered pot from Phaistos shown inset at left. The technical prowess of master potters culminated in eggshell ceramics thin enough to mimic metallic prototypes, as does the gracefully shaped cup below left. The same freedom of design informs the plan of the building itself.

The sophisticated sensibility revealed in objects found at Phaistos bespeaks a wealthy, cultivated court, whose members occupied elegant residential quarters incorporating a superb vista. Was this a summer residence for Knossos royalty? Or did rivals to the ruler of Knossos hold sway here? From the archaeological evidence, all that can be stated with any certainty is that the lords of Phaistos oversaw well-stocked storerooms, imposing public halls, ritual chambers, ample holding pens for animals, and the public ceremonies that would have been enacted in their expansive central and western courtyards.

*The well-preserved staircase below complemented the magnificence of Phaistos' monumental western facade. Its twelve 45-foot-wide stone risers provided a stately entrance to the palace. Carved into the stairs are snakelike channels, of unknown purpose, that meander down the steps.*

# LIFE FROZEN IN TIME
# UNTOUCHED BY PLUNDERERS

Perched at Crete's easternmost tip, surrounded by land poorly suited to the plow, Zakros faced seaward, a beneficiary of the rich trade with Syria and Egypt. The palace supported a sophisticated court and workshops notable for so-called Marine Style ware.

akros, the most recently excavated of the great Cretan palaces, lay unsuspected until a peasant's payment for lifesaving surgery brought it to light in the mid-20th century. In lieu of money, the local farmer gave his doctor, a knowledgeable antiquities collector, three objects unearthed in a field at Kato Zakros, each, like the bull's-head pendant inset below left, exquisitely crafted of pure gold. Word of this treasure reached the British archaeologist Nicholas Platon, who suspected a royal origin. In 1962 he found it.

Excavation disclosed an especially rich picture of daily life. Objects lay where their owners had left them the instant they fled the calamity of the 1470s. Beautiful pottery decorated in the Marine Style typical of the New Palace Period testified to the prowess of court artisans. Strikingly painted fish, octopuses, and shells, as on the vessel at left, showcased both the Minoans' artistic innovativeness and their detailed knowledge of sea life.

Indeed, the sea dominated life at Zakros, a palace that owed its wealth and power to the bustling harbor within sight of its upper windows. Envoys from distant powers bore gifts and messages. Palace storerooms bulged with exports and imports, while scribes kept meticulous accounts. Palace weavers, potters, carvers, and smiths crafted top-quality goods for a thriving trade carrying Minoan products as far as Egypt.

*Before their sacred rites, Evans believed, Minoans purified themselves in pools like the one below. Other scholars thought these were mere bathing areas. The stone amphora at right, of a type previously known only from pictures of rituals, was found smashed in the pool at Zakros; it argues strongly for Evans's theory that the basins served a sacred purpose.*

# A STUNNING CACHE AT A COUNTRY COURT

Set in the midst of a fertile coastal plain against a backdrop of Mount Dikte, the palace at Mallia commanded a large and diverse region rich in agricultural resources. Its site permitted it to expand more easily than Knossos and Phaistos, with their confining hilltop and valley locations. Thus the palace became the center of a loosely scattered urban nexus.

Mallia is about equal in size to the royal structure at Phaistos, with which it shares two features, its construction of local stone and its apparent lack of the wall paintings and architectural embellishments common at Knossos. In its plan and in the disposition of its rooms, however, Mallia parallels the other palaces with its central court, exterior court, shrine room, grand stairway, multiple storage rooms, and elaborate living quarters.

Reflecting its locale on the plain, Mallia had a rural character all its own. The agricultural bounty of the surrounding countryside, stored in eight large circular stone granaries and many storerooms lined with great oil- and grain-filled jars, formed the basis of its wealth.

The palace itself concealed far richer treasures. In an alcove behind a narrow stairway, archaeologists came upon a cache of ornate ceremonial weapons, including a bronze dagger with an engraved gold-plated hilt; a bronze sword with a handle of crystal and gold; and, stashed away in a pottery jar, the leopard-shaped stone ax head shown at right. Insignia of both elevated rank and sacral power, these arms must have adorned an august personage, perhaps a ruler who combined in the royal being the sacred and secular powers needed to preside over a royal establishment at once both palace and temple.

*Fifteen feet across, these stone granaries had plaster linings. One theory proposes that they were water cisterns, but their aboveground siting and resemblance to Egyptian silos argue to the contrary.*

*Alone among great Cretan palaces, Mallia retains essentially intact its ancient ground plan. Located close to the coast, it lay at the intersection of eastern and western routes carrying overland commerce and communication. Immense pithoi, once stuffed with valuables, hint at the palace's accumulated riches.*

*Caught in midleap, this leopard, carved from schist, formed the head of a ceremonial ax wielded by a palace official. With great cats no nearer than Syria, it testifies to Mallia's wide-ranging cultural contacts.*

# ENDURING GRANDEUR IN THE HEARTLAND OF POWER

The crowning glory of Cretan architecture and the hub of a metropolis of perhaps as many as 80,000 souls, the palace complex at Knossos sprawled over six acres, twice the area of Phaistos and Mallia and three times that of Zakros. Its innumerable rooms housed a vast aggregation of persons and activities. It also occupied a central place in Cretan religion, as is proclaimed by the "horns of consecration" *(below, right)* believed to represent bull's horns. Seen here as restored by Evans, they stand before the South Propylaeum, or entrance, through which ceremonial processions passed.

Over such majesty presided the mightiest potentate on this rich and cultured island; indeed, if ancient myth distills the truth, among the mightiest in this whole reach of the Aegean. The palace's mythic founder and Crete's most celebrated sovereign, Minos was—or so the Greeks believed—a son of their high god, Zeus. In its heyday, during the Old Palace and New Palace periods, Knossos befitted so august an antecedent. In design, decor, and furnishings, it expressed the artistic brilliance of a rich and sophisticated indigenous culture. During the Post-Palace Period, after the palace had risen a second time from the ruins, its paintings and artifacts embodied a new and foreign sensibility. The vessel at right, for example, bears the traditional Minoan double ax but displays a stylized formality more akin to the art of mainland Mycenae than to the bold naturalism that had so long exemplified the spirit of Crete. Taking into account this abrupt stylistic change and the fact that records began to be kept in Linear B, the language of the Mycenaeans, scholars suspect that mainlanders controlled Knossos in its final decades.

*Stashed among inscribed clay tablets, this impression left by a stone seal apparently portrays a Minoan dignitary. Seals bearing diverse symbols were used for administrative purposes throughout Crete.*

Mount Juktas, its contour supposedly embodying the profile of Zeus himself, looms over Knossos' vast expanse. A center of settlement at least since Neolithic times, this broad valley provided the Minoans with rich farmland, water sources more plentiful than today's, easy access to the best bay on the island's Aegean side, and control of the cross-Crete road to Phaistos and the south coast.

# A CONTROVERSIAL LOOK BACK AT A FABLED WAY OF LIFE

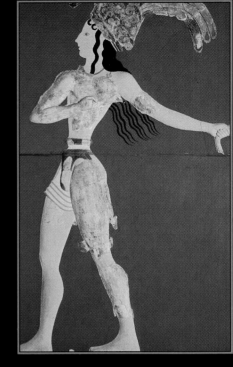

In his zeal to comprehend the life of the fabulous culture he had unearthed at Knossos, Evans went far beyond mere excavation. In a step that some later archaeologists have considered misguided and overbold, he rebuilt portions of the palace according to his own understanding of the Minoans' world. His reconstruction of the relief fresco at right, known as *Prince of the Lilies,* is now recognized as incorrect. Though the musculature looks masculine, its original white paint, traditional in images of women, suggests otherwise. Still, some scholars argue that, without Evans's reconstruction, the exposed ruins would have deteriorated badly and that although his "reconstitutions" occasionally erred, on the whole they present a useful, and strikingly accurate, picture of the elegant and dynamic life of the great palace. The brilliant political, cultural, and religious life of Homer's "mighty city" must surely have played itself out in rooms as impressive and richly appointed as those Evans envisioned.

*This majestic staircase of shallow gypsum steps connected the central court to the residential quarters. A masterpiece of Minoan architecture, it rises five flights toward a massive light well. The three lower flights and part of the fourth were found intact; the remaining portions were restored from the original blocks. Evans modeled the unusual, downward-tapering columns on fresco images.*

Evans dubbed this stately chamber, complete with its own private bathroom and stairway to the upper floor, the Queen's Megaron, or sitting room. He heavily reconstructed the celebrated Dolphin Fresco, to the skepticism of some experts.

At posts like this near the Grand Staircase, Evans inferred, soldiers guarded the approaches to the royal apartments. A reconstructed fresco of shields imparts a martial air to the surroundings.

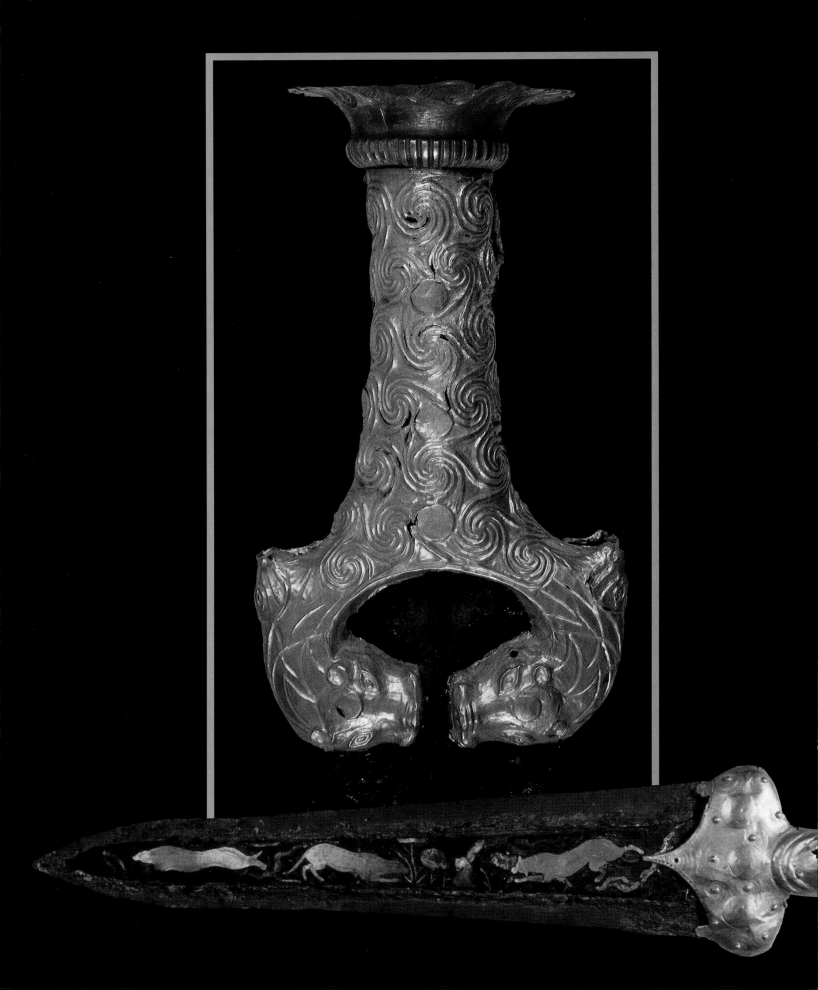

# MYCENAEAN GREECE: HOME OF THE HEROES

**F**or years a certain puzzling aspect of Mycenaean archaeology had intrigued Carl Blegen, a professor at the University of Cincinnati and one of the foremost experts on prehistoric Greece. In a section of Homer's *Iliad* known as the Catalog of Ships, there is a list of more than 30 rulers of independent Mycenaean kingdoms who took part in the Trojan War. Yet by 1939 only two of the palaces at the center of these kingdoms—Agamemnon's Mycenae and Diomedes' palace at Tiryns—had been excavated, both by Schliemann, while Oedipus' Thebes, buried beneath the modern town of Thivai, had been only tentatively probed. Searches for the palaces of Achilles, Menelaus, Odysseus, and other great heroes of the Trojan expedition had yielded no convincing clues.

The palace of Nestor, king of Pylos, who had sent the second largest fleet of ships against Troy, was thought to be located on the west coast of the Peloponnesus. But the exact location had been a matter of controversy since classical times, for there were three places that bore the name of Pylos along that coast.

Blegen's hunch was that Nestor's Pylos lay to the south, in the area of the Bay of Navarino. Several tombs of the form known as tholos—an underground structure of stone, constructed in the shape of a beehive and usually reserved for royal or noble dead—had been found to the north of the bay. This was a strong indicator that a major

*Mycenaeans took to the grave symbols of their power and wealth, as exemplified by the gold-sheathed hilt of a ceremonial sword and the inlaid blade of a dagger seen here.*

citadel may have existed in the vicinity, and the cove would have provided ideal sheltered water for a fleet.

"Sandy Pylos," Homer had called Nestor's great kingdom-by-the-sea. Nobody—not even Thucydides, the Greek historian—knew exactly where it was. But Blegen, who had directed an excavation at Troy between 1932 and 1938, had high hopes of finding out. In the spring of 1939, he began to explore the hills and ridges inland from the bay. From a short list of ancient habitation sites he chose as the most likely spot Ano Englianos, a defensible hill with an adequate source of water nearby and, protruding out of the ground, a large solid knob of what looked like limestone that had been roasted by fire sometime in the past.

The top of the steeply scarped hill formed a small plateau some 400 feet above sea level. It was a less dramatic site than the citadel at Mycenae or the acropolis in Athens, but it had a commanding view over every possible line of approach, and it was far enough from the sea to be safe from pirate attack, while near enough to operate ships from the open sandy beaches to the west or from the sheltered natural harbor of the Bay of Navarino, five miles distant. It was not hard to see why Mycenaeans of the Late Bronze Age might have raised a great palace on this site, so Blegen planned a spring dig.

At half past seven on the morning of April 4, 1939, the archaeologist and his assistant, William McDonald, then a student at the American School of Classical Studies at Athens, set off for Ano Englianos from their base in the modern town of Pylos. The weather did not look propitious for the start of their excavation. A chill wind was blustering in from the sea, and dark clouds glowered over the land, threatening rain before noon. It was only a short drive, but the winding road that led to the hill was a rough, bone-shaking one, for this was remote, rural country of rugged ridges and deep ravines, vineyards, and ancient olive groves, with the sea on one side and a mountain range on the other.

Arriving at the site, Blegen marked out a trench, about 54 yards long and two yards wide, and McDonald took charge of the digging. The first spade went in; barely a foot down, it struck something substantial. Observing with mounting interest, Blegen tersely recorded in his field notebook: "Looks like walls of big building. Earth black and red, all burned. Shards few."

By midmorning the excavators had uncovered the first of the site's historic finds—a seemingly nondescript clay fragment covered

*The Bay of Navarino, sheltered by the island of Sphakteria, is the biggest enclosed bay in the Mediterranean. As such, it probably served as the port for the nearby Mycenaean community of Pylos. Archaeologist Carl Blegen named the administrative center of Pylos the Palace of Nestor after the king in Homer's* Iliad, *a hero of the Trojan War.*

with a hard white accretion of lime. Noticing that the fragment had a rounded upper edge, one of the workmen picked up the object. Before anyone could stop him, he wiped his hand across the surface, revealing—and very nearly obliterating—a set of written symbols inscribed in the clay. Similar objects soon appeared, saturated with moisture and riddled with rootlets, their outlines barely distinguishable from the earth from which they had been formed.

Recalling the event some years later, McDonald wrote that the discovery was "the dramatic stuff of which movies are made but that seldom happens in the real context of slow, unexciting, uncomfortable, and often disappointing archaeological exploration. By incredible good luck the first trench exposed the ruins of a little room that still contained broken clay tablets inscribed in a writing system that seemed on first impression to be identical with Evans's 'Minoan' Linear B. So, here in Messenia, Blegen discovered the earliest cache of written records then known on the continent of Europe." These writings were destined to shed a completely new light on the mystery surrounding Mycenaean civilization.

During the following weeks, the initial trench was widened and many more clay tablets were gingerly prized from the ground. By the time the archive room was cleared, the inventory of tablets exceeded 600. Each was dried in the sun, photographed, sketched, numbered, wrapped in cotton wool, and taken to the team's house in modern Pylos. From there Blegen sent telegrams to Athens and Cincinnati to announce the momentous news.

He ordered seven further trenches dug to determine the parameters of the structure. These revealed a web of rooms and corridors indicating the existence of an extremely large building complex—almost certainly a great palace—still buried beneath the ground. It was clear to Blegen that the entire building had been destroyed in a great fire. That same fire had baked the clay tablets he had found there and thus preserved the writing. Fragments of pottery led Blegen to date the fire at about 1200 BC.

Meanwhile, about a half-mile south of the main site, some of Blegen's team found a tholos under a drying bed for currants. There workers uncovered many objects of gold, bronze, stone, ivory, and pottery, which had been overlooked during an ancient robbery. The total of royal burial places ultimately located in the immediate Pylos area totaled five, a number exceeded only by those at Mycenae.

By the end of his first season's dig, Blegen was confident he

# DECODING ANCIENT WRITINGS WITH WARTIME INTELLIGENCE METHODS

A host of scholars and amateur cryptologists have tried to decipher Aegean scripts ever since their discovery in the 19th century. Chief among the hobbyists was Michael Ventris, a British architect. In an astounding display of logic and insight, in 1952 he succeeded in decoding one of the ancient writings.

Ventris heard Sir Arthur Evans lecture when he was a boy; it sparked a lifelong infatuation with early Aegean cultures. After World War II, he devoted his spare time to deciphering Linear B, the Mycenaeans' written language, staying in touch with classical scholars as

he did so. Ventris used military code-breaking techniques, which taught him to look for recurring patterns. Linear B seemed to him a syllabic script in which each sign represented a consonant and a vowel, and a group of signs signified a word. Pictographs showing tradable commodities, such as horses, were interspersed with words in the text. Numerical symbols were easy to spot; they were collections of circles, lines, and dots, adding up to the digits they represented. Beside most of the numbers were words Ventris took to be nouns.

Swayed by the prevailing

view that Linear B was not Greek, Ventris long believed the writing an archaic Aegean tongue. But then, as a "frivolous diversion," he asked himself, "Might the language of these texts be Greek?"

Greek nouns end in vowels, and the vowels change depending on whether a word is the subject of a sentence, or a direct or indirect object. Ventris was able to identify three vowels because they were placed at the ends of words he assumed were nouns. He then deduced whether each of these nouns was the subject or object (direct or indirect) of its sentence.

Ventris next made a table with symbols sharing the same vowels in vertical columns and those sharing the same consonants written horizontally. Sometimes guided by pictographs appearing near words, he assigned Greek phonetic values to signs and sets of signs. As he manipulated the vowels and consonants in his table, Greek words began to emerge with increasing frequency. Ventris completed the decoding in collaboration with the classicist John Chadwick. A few weeks before his monumental work was published, he died, at the age of 34, in an auto crash.

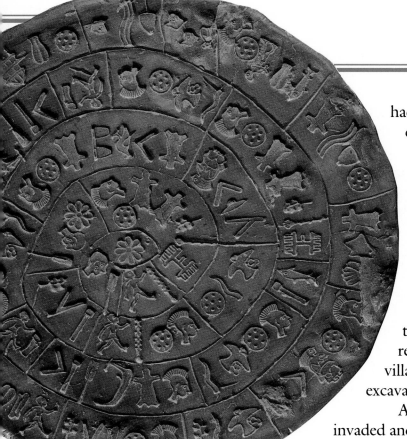

*A disk unearthed at the palace of Phaistos (above) may be the earliest example of printing; each of its signs was stamped onto clay with a seal. They depict humans, animals, vegetation, and ships. Six inches in diameter and nearly an inch thick, the piece was created before 1600 BC. It probably originated at Crete, or was brought there from one of the lands on the Minoan trade route.*

*The signs of Linear A (left) appear on a 3,500-year-old clay tablet from the archives at Hagia Triada, a Cretan villa. While its symbols are similar to those of Linear B, the words they create are in an unknown language that has defied translation. Below this script is one of the clay tablets Michael Ventris used in deciphering Linear B. Pictographs representing three-legged cauldrons validated his translation of the Mycenaean Greek word tripode. On the right are numerical signs that signify totals of objects.*

had solved at least part of the conundrum that had drawn him to the area, and in his preliminary report he announced: "We venture therefore without hesitation, even in these early phases of our investigation, to identify the newly found palace at Ano Englianos as the home of King Nestor, the 'sandy Pylos' of Homer and tradition."

When the dig ended in May 1939, workmen filled in the trenches so that local farmers could cultivate the land again. Many of the objects recovered, including the clay tablets, were taken to the National Museum in Athens to be cleaned and repaired; others were left in a storeroom in a nearby village. Blegen returned to Cincinnati to plan a major excavation of Pylos the following spring.

A few months later the world was at war. Greece was invaded and occupied, and Sir Arthur Evans's villa at Knossos was taken over for the German command center in Crete. Contact between Blegen and his Greek colleagues was severed. Fortunately, a complete photographic record of the Pylos tablets had reached Blegen in America before the outbreak of hostilities. Their transcription was long and painstaking, not helped by the archaeologist's entering military service. And still more years would elapse before the script in which they were written could be deciphered and their contents understood.

In the years after Blegen's spade bit into the remains of Nestor's palace, archaeologists would comb the region amassing a body of physical evidence that documented the rise and fall of this remarkable civilization. Blegen would continue his exploration of Pylos, the most completely preserved Mycenaean palace. Moreover, in a dramatic leap of ingenuity, a young Englishman, Michael Ventris, would decipher the script on the clay tablets found in Nestor's archive and elsewhere. Suddenly readable, these ancient writings would permit scholars to fill in many of the gaps in their understanding of this fascinating prehistoric world.

Seen as brawling, feasting, lusty individualists, these proto-Greeks had assumed a legendary status in the memory of later Greeks, who regarded the Mycenaean era as an age of heroes. Through archaeological detective work and under the probe of scholarship, they would turn out indeed to have had many of the characteristics that Homer attributed to them: They were exceptionally tall, well-built, and ambitious, with an appetite for armed conflict. Aggressive and expansionist, they adapted to their environment by dominating and developing it. Borrowing many elements of their culture from the Minoans, they developed Minoan ideas in their own way and added new notions. Most obviously, they adopted the concept of the great palace center and the system of bureaucratic control necessary to administer such communities, a system based on written records. Then they built their own palace complexes, which soon crowned the major citadels of Mycenaean Greece. These were grandiose structures, lavishly furnished, and perhaps meant to declare to all who arrived at the palace the wealth and power of the ruling dynasty.

World War II, and the Greek civil war that followed it, not only postponed excavation at Pylos for 13 frustrating years but also delayed the publication of the transcription of the tablets found there. Meanwhile, the only published material scholars had to work on was a limited number of transcripts of the Knossos tablets, and this meant, of course, that any progress in deciphering Linear B would be slow and tentative. With the publication of *The Pylos Tablets* in 1951, however, the first full and reliable list of signs became available. This was supplemented in the following year by complete transcriptions of the Knossos tablets in *Scripta Minoa II*, begun by Sir Arthur Evans and completed after his death by his friend Sir John Myres. The sudden appearance of this wealth of material was a spur to further efforts at decoding the ancient writing. Then, in 1952, two concurrent events happened that would change the perceptions most scholars held of the Mycenaeans: Blegen returned to Pylos to resume his excavations of Nestor's palace just as the first major breakthrough in solving the riddle of Linear B came in England.

Though incomplete, Blegen's first dig had produced an unsettling effect on scholars. Heinrich Schliemann's pioneer excavations at Mycenae and at Tiryns, which he explored shortly after his discovery of a Mycenaean civilization, had generated a considerable amount of subsequent archaeological investigation into prehistoric Greece; yet the picture of Mycenaean civilization was still fragmented. Most scholars accepted Sir Arthur Evans's theory that the Minoan civilization of Crete not only influenced the art and culture of the Mycenaean mainland but also dominated it in every other respect, even exercising political control of at least the major population centers. But the written tablets Blegen had recovered from the archive room at Pylos posed a problem.

It was clear that the writing on these tablets was virtually the same as the Linear B script found at Knossos during the excavations carried out by Evans. The problem was the chronology. The Knossos tablets seemed to have been inscribed about 1400 BC, when the palace was burned down and Minoan power came to an end. The Pylos tablets were dated nearly 200 years later. This could be interpreted as evidence that the Minoans had actually seized control of Mycenaean citadels before the eclipse of their native palaces in Crete, and were still in power on the mainland two centuries later. On the other hand, a major reevaluation might be needed. Evans believed the Pylos discovery meant that the Minoan rulers had moved their palace bureaucracy to the mainland, and he died feeling vindicated.

For more than 20 years, however, Blegen had held a contrary view. He thought that Mycenaean civilization represented a separate, independent society. The acid test could be the language of Linear B. The orthodox view was that Linear B represented an unknown Cretan tongue of non-Greek origin that had cropped up on the Greek mainland. But no one was sure because no one could read it.

This circumstance changed after Michael Ventris, a young English architect with a talent for languages who had been absorbed in the problem of Linear B as a gifted amateur cryptographer, made a historic radio announcement in June 1952. "During the last few weeks," he said, "I have come to the conclusion that the Knossos and Pylos tablets must be written in Greek—a difficult and archaic Greek, seeing that it is 500 years older than Homer and written in a rather abbreviated form, but Greek nevertheless. Although many of the tablets remain as incomprehensible as before, many others are suddenly beginning to make sense."

The idea was so unorthodox that reception was mixed, but unforeseen corroboration came quickly. Ventris, joining forces with John Chadwick, a classicist at Cambridge University, sent a paper on the deciphering to Blegen, which reached him as he was setting off for the second season of his dig at Pylos, in the spring of 1953. The new tablets, found the previous year, had been cleaned during the winter, and Blegen now began to try out the experimental syllabary, or syllable-based alphabet, outlined by Ventris and Chadwick.

What he saw was so astonishing that he wrote to Ventris at

once, enclosing a photo of one of the tablets, which, Blegen wrote, "evidently deals with pots." Next to the Mycenaean word *ti-ri-po-de*—nearly identical to the Greek word *tripode* from which the English word *tripod* is derived—stood an ideogram of three-legged cauldrons of the kind used for cooking and boiling in Mycenaean palaces. "The odds against getting this astonishing agreement purely by accident are astronomical," John Chadwick commented afterward, "and this was a proof of the decipherment which was undeniable." Greek was now shown to be the oldest continuous Indo-European language yet known.

In terms of the unraveling of the mysteries of Mycenaean civilization, the decipherment of Linear B *(page 122)* ranks with Schliemann's excavation of ancient Mycenae and Blegen's discovery of the Palace of Nestor at Pylos. The recovery of a small number of Linear B tablets and seal impressions at other palaces—Mycenae, Tiryns, and Thebes—confirmed that this early form of Greek was in use throughout Mycenaean Greece. But it was found only at palace centers, or at nearby locations that were dependent on palaces, suggesting that it was essentially a tool for keeping administrative accounts. This evidence, taken together with both the absence of the Minoans' Linear A on the mainland and the presence of Linear B at Knossos in the Post-Palace Period, proved conclusively that Minoan Crete, in its final phase, was under Mycenaean domination, not the other way around, as Evans had thought. Ventris, joining forces with Chadwick, who specialized in the early history of the Greek language, now prepared a full account of the tablets and what they had to say about Mycenaean life.

This pioneer interpretation of the tablets would be incomplete and in some respects conjectural. Partly this was because of the many obscure names and words whose precise meaning was unclear. But it was also because of the particular use of writing in Mycenaean culture. The Linear B tablets contain no private communications, no personal utterances by individuals, no letters, no memoirs, and no historical narratives. The writing was used exclusively for keeping tabs on the complex day-to-day transactions of an elaborately organized bureaucratic society—in the words of the British scholar Sir Denys Page, a society "divided and subdivided and labeled and inspected and rationed and in general controlled in all its phases by a restless and pervasive army of officials." Reflecting this, the tablets consisted solely of listings of people, religious activities, land

# A PANOPLY OF POWERFUL GODDESSES

From the preponderance of female effigies unearthed on Crete, it would seem that a Great Goddess dominated Minoan religious belief. She apparently presided over all of nature—every leafy bough and ripening field, creatures tiny and great, the bounty of the sea, the rumblings of the earth and air, and even fertility itself. Indeed, so ubiquitous was she and so strong her worship that the conquering Mycenaeans incorporated her, as they did many other Minoan elements into their culture, in their pantheon as a protector of herds, harvest, and household.

Whether she was a single deity or took several forms is impossible to determine, for no written texts exist to explain the thousands of years' worth of sculptures and other representations—several of which can be seen here and on the following pages—that portray her in a wide range of attire, shapes, and attitudes.

Crete was not alone in its adoration of such a goddess. Found at sites throughout the Aegean, sa-

tenure, livestock, agricultural produce, and manufactured articles.

Mycenaean scribes were reluctant to state the obvious: Nowhere did they record the name of the king or the collective name of the people. Homer spoke of them as Achaeans; the word *Hellenes* did not come into use until after Homer's time, and the word *Greek* derives from the Roman term for these early inhabitants. Archaeologists call them Mycenaeans today for convenience, after the name of their greatest palace.

Although only a fraction of the archives of a single year at Pylos have survived, they record thousands of transactions at hundreds of places, log a variety of details, and count, weigh, measure, and classify virtually every item of business, consequential and trivial. So in addition to recording the distribution of enough bronze to make 500,000 arrowheads or 2,300 swords, the assiduous scribes also duly noted the existence of a pair of bronze-bound chariot wheels at Pylos, which they labeled as "useless," and listed totals of sheep running into tens of thousands. They were not above recording the contribution of a single sheep by a single individual by the name of Komawens, the wheat and fig ration of 37 female bath attendants at Pylos, and the names of two oxen, "Glossy" and "Blackie," belonging to someone called Tazaro. "One would suppose," remarked one archaeologist, "that not a seed could be sown, not a gram of bronze worked, not a cloth woven, not a goat reared nor a hog fattened, without the filling of a form in the Royal Palace."

The tablets were essentially up-to-date files concerning very recent business. When they were manufactured, the clay was merely

cred figurines dating back some 8,000 years to the beginning of the Neolithic period are predominantly female, with swollen bellies and genitals that bespeak fertility goddesses or votive offerings to them. Male gods do not come to the fore until classical times, when Zeus and his pantheon gained ascendancy.

Some archaeologists think that on Minoan Crete a male deity assumed the role of divine son, born every spring to the Great Goddess in the form of new and regenerating flora. Yet when the Mycenaeans added to their holy roster a guardian of war—a dimension entirely absent from Minoan culture—they made her female, a likely precursor of Athena.

*Found in Thessaly, a realistically modeled clay figure from the fifth millennium BC emphasizes female fertility (1). Crafted between 2900 and 2600 BC, the clay "Goddess of Myrtos" (2) clasps a jug in her thin arms, perhaps signifying her dominion over the home; and from Pre-Palace Crete, a rhyton of a mother goddess appears to express milk from her breasts when fluids are poured from the vessel (3).*

1          2          3

sun-dried, scholars believe, not fire-baked; after their contents had been copied onto other, more permanent material—papyrus, perhaps, or skin—they were usually thrown into a vat of water and reformed as blank new tablets. So archaeologists have only been able to recover Linear B lists from palace centers like Pylos, which were burned down by fires that had baked the tablets hard enough to be preserved through the millennia that followed.

Despite their shortcomings, these jottings nonetheless reveal fascinating details about the organization of the Mycenaean kingdoms. A number of these details went some way toward filling in the blanks between the walls cleared by Blegen at Nestor's palace. While only one bathtub, for example, had actually been found in the palace, the tablets list three. And although no furniture survived the ravages of fire, time, and looters, the Pylos writings provide some idea of the royal cabinetmakers' art. One item, according to the American classical scholar Emily Vermeule, was so outrageously gaudy that the scribe who listed it on his inventory had some difficulty describing it. "A greenwood chair inlaid with blue glass paste and

*A faience statue in Minoan dress discovered in the palace at Knossos probably signifies the Great Goddess, fixing her intense gaze outward and holding aloft a pair of writhing serpents (4); while on the surface of a gold signet ring fashioned by a Minoan craftsman around 1550 BC, a trio of priestesses pay homage to a goddess among stylized blossoms (5). Decorated in the stylistic manner of Mycenaean pottery, a 13th-century BC statue of a goddess from Mycenae wears painted necklaces and bracelets (6).*

4       5       6

electrum and gold," he wrote, "the braces inlaid with gold men and stags' heads, gold bulls' heads, gold palm trees and blue glass-paste palm trees." Vermeule suggested that living with such a piece of furniture would have been nerve-racking, which may explain why the king seemed to have kept it locked in a storeroom.

The tablets also deal with the broader picture of power and economics in the kingdom, although again the picture is incomplete. The Mycenaean era on mainland Greece did not involve a single political entity or unified kingdom, still less a formal empire, but instead was broken up into dozens of rival kingdoms. Each of the principal regions had its central palace or citadel, independent of the next, ruled by its own rich and powerful aristocratic dynasty and managed by its own bureaucracy. From the citadels, tight control was maintained over the surrounding towns. The kingdom of Pylos, for example, had 16 towns, each in the charge of a governor and a local administrator, and was divided into a Hither Province and a Farther Province. Each of these provinces was subdivided into 16 districts.

The ruler of each region was the *wanax*, a title perhaps similar to the English word *king*. Apparently the wanax was the supreme

*Small pieces like this Mycenaean work of a woman cradling an infant in her arms (7), probably the Great Goddess in her role as nurturer and protector of children, have turned up throughout the eastern Mediterranean. Similarly, two female figures attend a child in a 13th-century BC ivory triad from Mycenae, perhaps a depiction of the goddess with nurse and child (8). Wearing a poppy headdress, a clay female figurine (ca. 1200 BC) unearthed near Herakleion on Crete (9) may reflect the power of healing or fertility dispensed by the divinity throughout the Aegean for centuries.*

7   8   9

authority in the political, economic, military, and religious spheres, reigning from his palace with the help of the *lawagetas,* a leader who may have been the commander in chief of the army. Among the king's minions were court officials who wore uniforms, may have owned slaves, and were known as *hequetai,* or king's followers. These members of the upper echelons of Mycenaean society were the principal landholders of the kingdom, along with another class in the social hierarchy, the *tereta,* landed barons who, as palace representatives, controlled the peasants on their estates and paid taxes to the wanax.

A marked feature of the palace work force was the specialization of labor, indicating a highly evolved manufacturing economy. The palace was not only the civil and military center of the region it controlled but the industrial and economic center as well. A huge staff of workers was needed to keep a palace complex like Pylos functioning smoothly. Within each craft were many subdivisions. There were masons, carpenters, architects, engineers, and shipbuilders. The armaments industry had its bowmakers and a host of specialists with an extensive knowledge of metallurgy who forged weapons. Some 270 bronzesmiths are listed at Pylos alone; a single category of bronzesmith made nothing but chariot wheels. Luxury

goods were created by goldsmiths, silversmiths, jewelers, ivory carvers, cabinetmakers, and perfumers, who heated olive oil with aromatic substances (sage and roses are mentioned). At the bottom of the social scale were slaves. Some 600 women recorded in the Pylos tablets seem to fall into this category, for many are called "captives"; in addition, a number of people are assigned menial tasks such as fetching water.

Agricultural production was also specialized, placed in the hands of shepherds, goatherds, cowherds, huntsmen, woodcutters, charcoal burners, and other types of rural workers. Although sheep were important at Pylos, flax and linen, rather than wool, were the main fibers. Grain, ground by women and

baked by men, was the staple food. Dairy products, olives and olive oil, figs, honey, wine, and a range of herbs and spices were all part of the diet of the Pylos region, and their collecting and preparation probably required yet another group of specialists.

There was no currency and no central market. Instead, the palace served as a center for manufacturing and redistributing goods,

*At left is a photo of Carl Blegen's excavation of the megaron, or throne room, in Nestor's palace at Pylos. A watercolor reconstruction* (above) *by Dutch illustrator Piet de Jong depicts the large, sumptuous room as it may have looked in the 13th century BC. The megaron, a structure common to all Mycenaean palaces, featured an enormous circular hearth surrounded by four columns. Frescoes adorned the walls, and even the ceilings and floors were plastered and painted.*

operations that must have been controlled by some form of rationing. Palace workers were compensated in kind, while tribute, from other towns in various districts, was paid in the form of commodities.

Besides shedding light on the economy, the tablets had much to say about religion, noting various gods as recipients of offerings, usually olive oil but also gold vessels. On one tablet, Poseidon is recorded as receiving one bull, four rams, cheese, wine, and honey, perhaps for a ceremonial feast. Revealed is a fully developed polytheistic religion complete with priests, priestesses, and cults. The only deities, however, that can easily be identified are ones whose names are familiar from legends of the later age of classical Greece—Zeus, Hera, Poseidon, Hermes, Athena, and Artemis. Several others are suggested, including perhaps a forerunner of Apollo and Ares, and possibly Dionysus. Religion clearly played a significant part in everyday life in Mycenaean Greece, but the tablets do not reveal the myths or doctrine behind the records.

No reference is made in the tablets to law, justice, crime, punishment, or coercion. Yet it is evident, from the massive construction projects undertaken at virtually every citadel, that considerable control had to be exerted over the population to conscript a labor force, diverting the workers from normal activities. More surprising, no data concerning trade and commerce with the rest of Mycenaean Greece and the outside world is found in the tablets. Nor is there anything that illuminates the epics of Homer, composed 400 years later but believed to refer back to this era. Nonetheless, the decipherment of Linear B, for all that it failed to reveal, was a marvelously enlightening achievement. "It has provided the dumb monuments of prehistoric Greece with a linguistic commentary," John Chadwick summed up, "incomplete and obscure, but a guarantee that their makers were Greeks. It has pushed back seven centuries the date of the earliest Greek inscriptions, and thus extended our knowledge of the Greek language, which now has a continuous recorded history, totaling thirty-three centuries."

The excitement generated by the decoding of Linear B distracted public and scholarly attention from Blegen's excavation of the Palace of Nestor. He had resumed his dig on May 30, 1952, shortly before Ventris's radio announcement. Blegen was 65 years old; he would be 77 before he finished this last great labor of his life. But his enthusiasm and his meticulous expertise were undiminished.

The new trench sunk by Blegen exposed the state rooms at the heart of the palace complex—the megaron, or throne room, together with the vestibule and portico that fronted it. The megaron was revealed as a large enclosed room measuring 42 by 37 feet. On the floor in the middle, Blegen found a great circular hearth where an open fire would have burned, and the bases of four tall fluted wooden columns. These would have supported the balcony of the second story and an elevated ventilation section of the roof. Small windows in the sides of the extended structure permitted smoke from the hearth to be vented.

Against the east wall, Blegen uncovered a hollow in the plastered floor that marked where the king's throne had stood before it was burned in the fire that destroyed the palace. From the debris in the megaron he retrieved fresco fragments that had fallen off the wall behind the throne—pieces of lions, griffins, a jug, men seated at a table, a lyre player seated on a rock, and a crested white bird flying through the air. The floor of the throne room was made of compacted clay coated in plaster and divided into squares painted with a variety of designs. The square in front of the throne was decorated with a stylized octopus, which might have been a royal emblem. Staircases led to rooms on the second floor.

Season after season the dig progressed, exposing a complex of corridors, storerooms, pantries, passages, cubicles, stairways, courtyards, waiting rooms, and a suite of apartments, including one assumed to be the queen's megaron. By 1956, the main palace building had been entirely cleared. Little identifiable treasure was found among the remains, for the most precious objects probably had been carried away by the fleeing inhabitants or looted by attackers at the time of the palace's destruction. The few small articles of gold, silver, bronze, ivory, bone, and paste uncovered by Blegen and his team had been damaged almost beyond recognition by the intensity of the fire.

Storerooms at the back of the megaron contained a number of large jars for holding olive oil, which would have fueled the final fire. Pantries and other storerooms were found to be full of household pots, some 6,000 in all, including nearly 3,000 stemmed drinking cups that had been stacked on wooden shelves and had smashed to the floor when the shelves went up in flames.

*A large bathroom where visitors might cleanse themselves, unique in its refinement, was located adjacent to one of the entrances to Nestor's palace. Its terra-cotta tub, enclosed in clay and plaster painted with spiral motifs, had a step to help bathers in and out and a built-in ledge to hold a sponge or toiletries.*

Of the items recovered from the palace building, the most important probably were objects made from clay; 468 more tablets and fragments were found in an annex to the archives. By the time the excavations were completed, the number of tablets recovered from the palace amounted to almost a thousand.

One of the most intriguing discoveries in Nestor's palace was a well-appointed bathroom next to the palace entrance. It is the only complete example yet found at a Mycenaean site. Its terra-cotta bathtub was set in a plaster surround and provided with a step, a ledge that may have been a sponge rack, and two clay goblets shaped like champagne glasses, which may have been used to pour water or oil on the bather. There was no hole in the tub; the water had to be bailed out and poured down a drainage conduit.

In the corner of the room stood two large jars. One may have held water, the other, perfumed olive oil; both were used for cleansing the body in ancient times. Attached by a connecting corridor to the secondary megaron is a room with a painted stucco floor, in which Blegen uncovered a drain for what he assumed to be a rudimentary toilet. It empties into an underground drainage system that connects different areas of the palace.

Turning his attention to the other buildings, the archaeologist saw that, like other Mycenaean palaces, the main structure was surrounded by a complex of ancillary buildings—wine stores, armories, stables, workshops, and warehouses. The town had spread over the hillside below the plateau on which the palace was located. At the bottom of one of the slopes, Blegen made a breathtaking find—3,000 fragments of Old Palace Period frescoes that had been dumped over the edge of the acropolis when the structure was renovated. Some of these, pieced together, form part of a nautilus shell, while others depict bluebirds; another group shows figures in a procession.

Unlike other great palaces, such as Mycenae or Tiryns, Pylos had no defensive wall. It did, however, have a good all-around view of the approaches and precipitous slopes beneath its acropolis. With no water source of its own, the palace had to pipe its supply through a wooden aqueduct from a spring on a neighboring hill. Protective walls that did not enclose the water supply, Blegen reasoned, would have been fairly useless. More significantly, Pylos was the center of a large, but geographically isolated, kingdom. Most of the fortified sites, such as Mycenae and Tiryns, were either situated close to one another or were relatively small entities. Since the kingdom covered a large area, the rulers of Pylos may have been more concerned with defending their overall territory than the palace.

Meanwhile, throughout Greece, there was an explosion of archaeological activity. New discoveries at Mycenae, Athens, Thebes, Iolcus, Tiryns, Orchomenus, Asine, Argos, Thorikos, and Marathon unearthed more of the physical structure of the Mycenaean world. By applying some of the analytical techniques developing in the discipline of anthropology, a few scholars of the Mycenaean period began to reinterpret the evidence produced earlier by field archaeologists. The palaces were now seen as having been more than the abodes of kings. They had a secondary purpose—to convey, through their imposing architecture, an unmistakable statement about the royal dignity and overwhelming power of the wanax.

Scholars now asserted that the megaron, which followed a broadly similar design in the palaces of Pylos, Mycenae, Tiryns, and Thebes, was more than just the biggest room in the palace; it was the architectural climax of a ranked series of rooms leading to the core of royal power. Inside, the secular power of the king was conveyed by the four columns, the large hearth, and the throne against the east wall; his religious standing was emphasized by the themes of the wall frescoes. Symbols of the mystic world, such as the griffins painted on the plastered surface behind the throne, conveyed a direct connection—over and above the ranks of the priesthood—between the king and the supernatural sphere.

The subtle meanings in the elaborate interior were aimed at the narrow audience of the elite. But the monumental grandeur of the palace exterior, like that of the Mycenae acropolis, or citadel, projected a public symbolism that signaled strength and permanence to the widest possible audience—and especially to the rival kingdoms of mainland Greece. Some scholars have suggested that the Mycenaean dynasts may have competed with one another to build the most impressive citadels and live in the most lavishly decorated palaces. These structures seem eloquent testimony to the assertion of the

*The perimeter of the ancient citadel of Mycenae is outlined by its defensive walls in an aerial view of the acropolis. Within the fortifications, the prominence of Grave Circle A and the palace center indicates their importance. Modest structures to the right of Circle A and beyond the palace housed artisans and retainers and served as workshops and storerooms.*

*The so-called Cyclopean construction of the citadel of Tiryns is most dramatic in its corbeled corridors built between the palace walls. The colossal fortifications of Tiryns, as at nearby Mycenae, are 30 feet high and 27 feet thick in some places. The early Greeks believed that the walls were built by the giants called Cyclopes.*

individual personalities of Mycenaean rulers, a trait that contrasts with the more communally minded culture of Minoan Crete. And, in their projection of might and achievement, they were no doubt a source of pride to the people themselves.

This urge to express wealth and power architecturally also seems inherent in the monumental, splendidly decorated and furnished tombs in which these rulers were finally laid to rest. At Mycenae, for example, the early custom of laying the royal dead at the bottom of deep shaft graves had been abandoned, once the palaces were built, in favor of a different form of interment—the tholos. This stone vault, built below ground level, was an impressive edifice. It was approached by a long walled passage cut into the slope of the hill.

The most magnificent example of a tholos is the so-called Treasury of Atreus, named after the Mycenaean king of later Greek legend. In sheer size it has no rival. The dome is nearly 50 feet in diameter and 43 feet from floor to ceiling, and the entrance is 17 feet high. In splendor it was no less impressive. With its cut and polished conglomerate, or mixed-stone, facade, it was flanked by two elaborately ornamented two-story columns of a green stone. In the upper story, a veneer of beams with carved glyphs was surmounted by a spiralform design of red stone. Both red and green stones were imported from Laconia, 60 miles southwest of Mycenae. The lintel of the tomb is a single slab of conglomerate weighing an estimated 120 tons. Every block of the vault is cut into a curved shape, and each course of stones decreases in size as the structure rises higher, until the blocks come together with meticulous precision in a flat stone at the top, a technique known as corbeling. The dome of this supremely prestigious resting place is still as sound and watertight as the day it was built, some 3,300 years ago.

Ever since 1876, when Schliemann sank his first trench into the citadel at Mycenae, scholars have asked certain fundamental questions. Who were these people who had suddenly risen to wealth and power? Did they come from Crete, as Evans believed? Were they invaders from the north, as some suggested because a portion of their artifacts seem to link them with the Balkans and Europe? There were archaeologists who argued that they may have originated in the Near East, bringing with them the chariot. Or, asserted another faction, they simply may have been indigenous mainlanders.

Questions of origin remain unanswered, but after decades of fieldwork and archival research, an approximate historical sequence of the Mycenaean world has been worked out. The oldest group of high-status burials at Mycenae was excavated in the 1950s by the Greek Archaeological Service. This was the so-called Circle B, which lay outside the acropolis and has now been dated to about 1550 BC. A ring of shaft graves, it is quite different from the elaborate tholos style that emerged during the period of the palaces. There are 24 burials in Circle B, most of them simple, traditional, and poorly furnished; five of them, however, contained a great deal of wealth. The grave goods recovered from the Circle B burials—gold and silver vessels; bronze weapons; a death mask made of electrum, a gold and silver alloy; and an exquisite rock-crystal bowl with a handle in the shape of a duck's head—showed, in their richness and artistry, a marked advance beyond the mainland Bronze Age norm of the time. The royal shaft graves excavated by Heinrich Schliemann in 1876, known as Circle A, are now considered to be of more recent date, roughly 1600 to 1450 BC, and mark yet another leap forward in Mycenaean wealth and sophistication. The next stage was the pinnacle of Mycenaean culture, the period of the grand palaces, during the 14th and 13th centuries BC, when royalty abandoned the shaft graves for the tholoi.

*One of the earliest tholoi on mainland Greece is the so-called Tomb of Thrasymedes. Thrasymedes was the son of Nestor, whose palace was nearby. Most of the tholoi, stone vaults built for the interment of the royal dead, were plundered long ago. A sacrificed ox was among the remains found in this tomb.*

*Imposing today, the tholos known as the Treasury of Atreus was even more impressive when first built in Mycenae in the 13th century BC. Green marble columns with zigzag fluting flanked the 17-foot-high doorway leading into the tomb* (left). *Slabs of ornately carved colored marble lined the area above the lintel. Nail holes remain where bronze rosettes ornamented the interior* (above).

Around 1450 to 1400 BC, the Mycenaeans, established throughout the mainland and with longstanding contacts on the islands, launched themselves on a century of overseas expansion. The crucial event on the road to domination was the conquest of most of the major sites in Minoan Crete, culminating in the occupation of Knossos around 1450 BC. The Mycenaeans were thus able to appropriate the Minoans' near monopoly of art and commerce in the Aegean, along with their technological know-how and artistic brilliance in metalwork, pottery, jewelry, and gem and ivory carving.

During the 14th and 13th centuries BC, the thriving Mycenaean palace kingdoms developed their economies by acquiring raw materials from overseas and creating markets for their own produce. Hitherto the Minoans had been the great maritime power in the region, but after the fall of Knossos the Mycenaeans took over, expanding their commercial networks with great rapidity throughout the region and replacing not only Minoan products but the Minoans themselves.

Mycenaean exports included olive oil and refined oil for perfumes, wool, linen, bronze swords, daggers, and double-headed axes, in addition to archaeologically untraceable goods like wine, textiles, timber, and even mercenary soldiers. But the commodity most visible to archaeologists today is the superbly made and beautifully decorated Mycenaean pottery *(page 145),* which was in constant demand all over the Mediterranean region. By tracking finds of surviving Mycenaean pottery, archaeologists have charted a wide-ranging system of trade within the Mediterranean, the Near East, Egypt, and Europe. So widespread was Mycenaean maritime trade in its heyday that many historians have concluded that the Mycenaeans were absolute rulers of the sea, controlling the shipping routes and treating the eastern Mediterranean as a virtual Mycenaean lake. It is not clear, however, whether the distribution of Mycenaean products represents the activities of Mycenaean, Cypriot, or Near Eastern merchants.

From the beginning, Mycenaean power had been based in large part on the military prowess of a fighting aristocracy. Mycenaean art contains abundant scenes of armed combat, while Mycenaean history and legend, as portrayed in the later epic poetry of Homer, is often about little else. By the 13th century BC, the Mycenaean armed forces had achieved a high degree of technical sophistication and combat effectiveness, with an infantry equipped with swords, daggers, spears, and battle-axes, and with support units in

# OF ARMS AND THE MAN: MYCENAEAN WARRIORS ON THE BATTLEFIELD

"These were the strongest generation of earthborn mortals," wrote Homer of the Mycenaeans, a militaristic people whose innovative "weapons of terror" were both feared and revered by those with whom they engaged in combat. Bursting onto the battlefield in chariots, the heroes of his epic poems brandished great spears and swords while deflecting blows with metal shields, protective armor, and boar's-tusk helmets. But were these tales true? After all, the Mycenaeans were long gone by the time Homer immortalized them.

The answer is yes, given the archaeological evidence. In the royal tombs at Mycenae, for example, a plethora of bronze weaponry has been unearthed. Many graves yielded the private arsenals of noblemen, including up to a dozen richly decorated swords and daggers as well as pikes, knives, spearheads, and arrowheads. Of these the warrior almost certainly would have carried into combat a three-foot-long sword for striking at his foe and a dagger for closer, cut-and-thrust

fighting. On occasion he might have used a pike to penetrate the enemy's armor.

Missing from the graves are the massive Mycenaean shields that protected the men from chin to ankle. Made of layers of ox hide, they perished ages ago. But images of them have survived, as can be seen on the dagger pictured below. The same is true of the wicker war chariot, captured on vases, sealstones, and steles, and mentioned in clay tablets found at Pylos and Knossos. These written records catalog the contents of the palace armory, where a fighting force of 200 chariots was maintained. Also listed is the heavy armor issued to charioteers, like the bronze suit seen at far right.

*A Mycenaean sealstone* (above) *and an impression taken from it show a warrior riding fully armored aboard a light, maneuverable wicker chariot and wielding a long spear. A driver did the steering.*

*Inlays of gold, silver, and black niello on this bronze blade re-create a dramatic moment in a lion hunt. Vanquishing their prey with javelins and a bow, the hunters are shown using two types of Mycenaean shields: the figure-eight shape and the oblong towerlike design. Inlaid daggers, owned by royalty—even princesses—were apparently worn at ceremonies.*

The headgear at far right, reconstructed from fragments recovered from a burial at Dendra, and the helmet in the ivory relief at right are both examples of boar's-tusk helmets. Up to 40 pairs of tusks were sewn onto a leather cap to make a single helmet. Out of the same grave came the bronze armor, a rare example that eluded robbers. Such equipment would have been owned by only the noblest of warriors.

Unlike their chieftains, the rank and file in the late Mycenaean period, ca. 1200 BC, wore the lighter leather corselets and horned helmets that are seen on this vase. Bulky body shields had been replaced by smaller, round shields more suitable for collective combat. The spear, however, remained an important infantry weapon.

the form of archers and slingshot troops. For defense, some Mycenaean soldiers carried long rectangular "tower" shields or smaller, figure-eight-shaped shields. Their enemies also faced the two-man, two-wheeled chariots, drawn by two horses, that packed a punch in the Mycenaean war machine.

Military aggrandizement broadly coincided with the high-water mark of political power and economic prosperity in Mycenaean Greece. The large number of settlements shows that the population of Greece had never been so dense, and would not be so again for another eight centuries. The standard of living of the mass of the population probably was at its highest ever, the power of its rulers unsurpassed. At Mycenae the defensive wall was extended to include more of the acropolis area, and a whole complex of workshops and commercial premises was constructed both outside and inside the walls. It was in this heyday, 1340 to 1250 BC, that great new palaces were built at Tiryns and Pylos, as well as a vast new acropolis at Gla, on an island in a lake northwest of Thebes.

Like other great states in ancient history, Mycenae declined and slipped into a dark age. Around the mid-13th century, Gla and Zygouris, which is north of Mycenae, apparently were destroyed by fire. During this same period, there seems to have been widespread unease. The rulers of major centers like Mycenae, Tiryns, and Athens took steps to include their water-supply systems *within* their defensive walls, and at Tiryns these fortifications were greatly expanded.

The cause of this mounting insecurity may have arisen partly as a result of anxiety over the intentions of other palace centers, especially as the pressure mounted on available resources, although this is a controversial view. It was the norm in Mycenaean Greece for each regional capital to regard itself as an independent power in its own right, both envious and fearful of its neighbor. Later Greek legends cite numerous examples of raids by one Mycenaean kingdom against another. Occasionally the more aggressive realms would come together in larger expeditions to mount concerted campaigns, such as the alleged venture against Troy—perhaps the last collective paroxysm of Mycenaean military might.

*A nearly life-size plaster head found in the ruins of a dwelling in Mycenae is unusual for its three-dimensional form. The sculpture's brightly painted but chilling countenance may be the likeness of a sphinx, with the head of a woman and the body of a lion. The dots on her cheeks and chin are reminiscent of early Cycladic figurines with painted faces.*

*A duck's head, so lifelike it might be preening its feathers, serves as the handle for a spouted bowl. Carved from a piece of rock crystal, the six-inch-long bowl is from a Circle B shaft grave at Mycenae. It may have been used to hold offerings.*

Archaeological evidence of the collapse of Mycenaean civilization is fragmentary, inconclusive, and hotly debated. Various causes—or combinations of causes—have been put forward to explain its eventual disappearance: civil war, social revolution, or slave revolt; foreign invasion by land or by sea; disruption of trade with the east, followed by interruption of grain imports leading to famine; climatic change (either too dry or too wet and cool for growing crops); disastrous epidemics; erosion caused by deforestation; and natural catastrophe such as a series of earthquakes.

Whatever the reason, various Mycenaean settlements were demolished in the second half of the 13th century BC. This was followed, at the beginning of the 12th century BC, by the destruction of great centers like Mycenae, Tiryns, Dendra, and Krisa, and the abandonment of a number of others. Smaller provinces like Prosymna were burned or deserted. There is evidence that the widespread destruction was perhaps the consequence of ripples from a more distant and universal disaster now overwhelming not only the Mycenaean world but much of the eastern Mediterranean from the Near East to Italy as well. In coastal Asia Minor, the Near East, and North Africa, the established civilizations of the Bronze Age were everywhere tottering. The Egyptian and Hittite empires had begun to lose their grip after the early 13th century BC.

As a result, frontier stability crumbled, inland tribes shifted their ground, and waves of desperate tribespeople, driven perhaps by population pressure and hunger, swept southward out of the Balkans and Transcaucasia, through Hittite lands, and down the Canaanite seaboard toward the Egyptian frontier, ravaging the cities and destroying the commercial centers by land and sea. At the same time, the so-called Sea Peoples, whose identity is one of the great mysteries of the Late Bronze Age, were active in the area. The Sea Peoples were not a single culture or race, but were rather mixed ethnic groups displaced from their homelands and sometimes loosely allied with the great powers. For years they ravaged the eastern Mediterranean seaboard and sea lanes.

It may have been the Sea Peoples whom the scribes at the ill-fated Pylos palace had in mind when they recorded on their clay tablets certain dispositions in the defenses of the Pylos coastal perimeter. According to the most favored, but still controversial, scenario of the archaeologists, Pylos was in a state of high military alert during the time the tablets were being inscribed. The threat appears

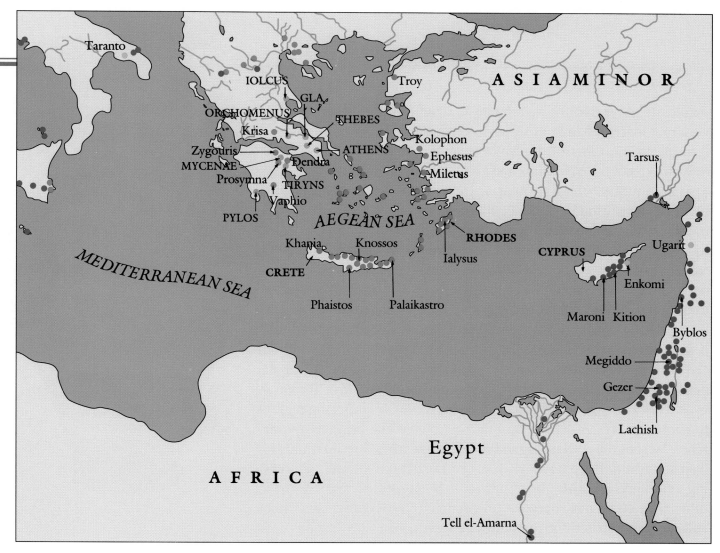

Map labels:

Taranto

IOLCUS

GLA

ORCHOMENUS

THEBES

Krisa

Zygouris

MYCENAE

Prosymna

Dendra

TIRYNS

Vaphio

PYLOS

ATHENS

AEGEAN SEA

Khania

Knossos

CRETE

Phaistos

Palaikastro

Troy

ASIA MINOR

Kolophon

Ephesus

Miletus

RHODES

Ialysus

Tarsus

CYPRUS

Ugarit

Enkomi

Maroni Kition

Byblos

Megiddo

Gezer

Lachish

MEDITERRANEAN SEA

Egypt

AFRICA

Tell el-Amarna

*Following in the wake of the Minoans, the Mycenaeans established colonies and trading partnerships around the Mediterranean. In the 14th and 13th centuries BC, their sphere of influence expanded to include southern Italy, Cyprus, Asia Minor, Syria, and Egypt. Here, the gold dots mark their palaces on the Greek mainland, and the red dots stand for Mycenaean settlements around the Aegean. The purple dots indicate places where Mycenaean remains have turned up, while green dots show sites of actual Mycenaean trading stations.*

to have come from the sea, though in exactly what form was never recorded. A number of defense stations had been established up and down the hundred miles of coastline. Sometimes the placenames were recorded on the tablets, along with the numbers of lookouts (approximately 800 men) and oarsmen available for posting to the fleet (about 600 of these).

The tablets also may have referred to the disposition of soldiers, concentrated mainly in the area nearest to the palace but also distributed along the coast and in the outlying districts under the command of the officers of the royal court. These references to military defenses may mean that a state of emergency was in force at the time the tablets were inscribed.

It is unlikely that there is a single cause for the collapse of the Mycenaean world. In all probability, there was a combination of causes. Banditry at sea and on land, and violent upheavals at the periphery of the Mycenaean empire could have effectively shattered trade links between Mycenaean Greece and the East, disrupting the wholesale movement of merchandise, depriving the Mycenaeans of vital raw materials such as tin and copper, and undermining the centralized economy of the Mycenaean palace centers. Tragically, this paralysis in foreign trade would have coincided with a maximum Mycenaean population pressing on the food supply. The disruption of imports of raw materials, and possibly of bulk foodstuffs such as grain, would almost certainly have led to a crisis, with many people going hungry. A series of crop failures might have diminished stores kept as a margin in times of need, deprived the populace of their staple food, and also seriously undermined industrial production and the trade that depended on it.

If the palace bureaucracy had been unable to respond adequately to the crisis, the elite class might have lost control. Without central guidance there was probably no way local communities, dependent on the palaces, could have coped on their own. Recovery would have been difficult and raids on better-off neighboring regions the only option. "An attack on a nearby town could bring temporary relief," wrote the archaeologist Philip Betancourt, "but it would also displace additional persons and add to the general disaster, disrupting trade and creating more havoc." He suggested that "flight to other areas could have been the only remaining alternative, with raids and coastal destructions the natural consequence."

Whatever the reason, it is clear that from about 1250 to 1190 BC the Mycenaean palace system of government suffered a more or less sudden death and disappeared forever, while the postpalace culture that was left succumbed to slow asphyxiation.

With the end of the great palace centers vanished the arts of carpentry, masonry, writing, fresco painting, and the carving of ivory and stone. Starting in the early 13th century BC, some forms of pottery gradually ceased to share a common Mycenaean style. In the 12th century BC, distinctive regional variations developed increasingly as the common culture disintegrated.

Over a 50-year period, the structure of the Mycenaean world underwent an irreversible change: One after another acropolis was abandoned. Although the mainland was never totally depopulated, the majority of the survivors seem to have turned their backs on the land and moved away in a Mycenaean diaspora that took them to the outer fringes of the Greek world—the coast and the islands.

Into the illiterate, leaderless land, moving slowly southward in bands out of the mountainous, barbarian north, came simpler folk

*The three vessels above illustrate both differences and similarities in Minoan and Mycenaean pottery. They all display forms common in the Aegean Late Bronze Age, and all are decorated with squid or octopuses, a popular motif. These mollusks, their flexible shapes well suited to vase painting, first appeared on pottery from Crete. The Minoan flask (center) features a realistic specimen, tentacles writhing. The Mycenaean tendency toward artistic formality shows in the vase at left. A crater, or mixing bowl, from Mycenaean Cyprus (right) is further simplified, its multiarmed subject stylized almost to abstraction.*

with inferior skills and lower expectations. These probably were the Dorians of legend. They too spoke a form of Greek but had more in common with the rougher tribes of the Balkans and central Europe than with the cultured Mycenaeans over whose abandoned farmlands they now wandered. Camping in the ruins of the deserted palaces, sheltering their livestock inside the huge walls of a civilization at the end of its tether, the new inhabitants took over the once-great Mycenaean realm not so much by force of arms—archaeology has found no evidence of fire and destruction at the time of their coming—but by the simple physical occupation of the sparsely inhabited former kingdoms. The Dorians did not cause the collapse of the Mycenaean empire; they simply took advantage of the prevailing circumstances that brought it about. As far as we can tell, they left no archaeological trace except possibly a coarse, burnished pottery.

The passing of the Mycenaeans by the 11th century BC spelled the end of the Bronze Age and the beginning of the Iron Age. Over mainland Greece and the islands, a dark age descended that was to last as long as 400 years. The Mycenaean survivors disappeared as an identifiable society, so that in time no one had any personal memory of what a Mycenaean looked like, dressed like, or talked like.

What did survive was the Mycenaean legacy. In purely material terms this did not add up to much, consisting as it did mainly of ruins of the citadels, including fortifications, gates, and building walls. The Mycenaeans also left some of their tombs, especially the great tholoi; the later inhabitants discovered some of these tombs and their contents when they plowed their fields or when the tomb chambers collapsed. It is also possible that the Mycenaeans passed on important genealogies of the major families at Mycenae, Athens, and Sparta, which became the substance of great legends.

The Mycenaeans and the Minoans bequeathed to later Greeks some aspects of their religion that would become important components of classical Greek culture. More important, they contributed to posterity their language, probably in the form of poetry, myth, and legend; it would form the bedrock of much of the literature and art of the great classical culture that was to flower in the Mycenaeans' wake—the starting point of Western civilization itself.

With writing forgotten, nothing was recorded during the long, blank centuries of the Dark Ages. But throughout that chasm of time, local tradition and wandering bards kept alive the distant memory of the once-mighty Mycenaeans and their great palaces and deeds of glory. The bards' oral tradition of poetry passed on, from one generation to the other, a dim memory of not only the heroics but also the names, and even the geography, of the misty Mycenaean past. In the eighth century BC this faint recollection—hazy, distorted, and muddled together with myths of the gods, but a memory nonetheless—was to burst upon a new and literate civilization in the form of Homer's monumental written epics, and in the rest of the great corpus of Greek mythology. For millennia, it would be the world's only nonarchaeological link with the golden age of Mycenaean civilization.

# A BRONZE AGE TIME CAPSULE

Some 3,300 years ago, a 40-foot-long trading vessel sailed west along Turkey's southern coast, probably bound for the Aegean. Following the eastern Mediterranean's circular trade route, the ship had taken on glass ingots and aromatic resins in Canaan, tin in Syria, and about 20,000 pounds of copper ingots in Cyprus.

Caught by a sudden and unusual shift of wind, she was forced onto the rocky face of a cape today called Ulu Burun. She was stoutly built, her two-inch-thick fir planks snugly mortised and pinned together by oak pegs, but the seas soon poured in. She plunged almost immediately to the sloping seabed 140 to 170 feet below, settling there. Her hull was gradually eaten away by shipworms, scattering valuable wood for furniture making, bronze chisels, drill bits, and axes, ingots, several bronze razors, and nine huge clay jars, one full of pomegranates. It is unknown if anyone escaped.

There the wreck sat for more than 3,000 years, undisturbed except when a Byzantine ship snagged an anchor on a pile of ingots and lost it. Then, one day in 1982, a Turkish diver named Mehmet Çakir, swimming the bottom for sponges, saw strange objects he later described as "metal biscuits with ears." Çakir's captain had been told by archaeologists from the Institute of Nautical Archaeology (INA) at Texas A&M University what to watch for underwater. He instantly realized the diver had found ancient four-handled ingots, like the one in the picture above.

Divers from INA soon photographed and sketched the site, and in 1984 a full-scale dig was launched. Operations would continue for years, but the incredible wealth of knowledge the discovery offered was evident from the outset. Declared INA director George F. Bass when he first saw pictures of the wreck, the world's oldest: "We are looking at an archaeologist's dream." As the following pages show, however, turning dream to reality was to be an arduous, even perilous task.

# A BUSY AND DANGEROUS WORKPLACE

The sea would not easily yield the secrets it had hidden for so long. Some of the scattered cargo lay about 190 feet below the surface—a distance equal to the height of a 19-story building. The great pressure at such depths can cause the bends as well as impaired judgment from increased nitrogen levels. "Every 50 feet of depth," said Bass, "produces in a diver the sensation of drinking an additional gin martini."

To reduce risk on these dives, seabed working time was limited to 20 minutes. The INA's research vessel provided an added safety stop: a double-lock recompression chamber for easing potential victims out of the bends. One of the first pieces of equipment to go down was the "phone booth," an air-filled Plexiglas™ dome into which a diver could duck for safety or to communicate with the ship overhead.

Soon there followed a long hor-izontal bar and cameras to use in "stereophotogrammetric mapping" of the site; an item's precisely plotted location could later be crucial to solving a historically significant puzzle. Vacuum pipes called airlifts helped remove sediment from finds, and air-filled balloons hoisted heavy loads to the surface.

For all the ingenious equipment, however, most of the dig still came down to hard, patient work. Divers had to abandon the use of small air-powered chisels, for instance, because they endangered fragile items; chipping and scraping continued by hand. On one occasion three divers spent more than two months on an area approximately two yards square. But the reward was a swelling horde of recovered archaeological treasures.

*The INA's 65-foot-long research vessel* Virazon *hovers over the wreck, providing power, communication, air, and protection to the divers below.*

*Donald Frey, INA photographer, positions a camera on a horizontal bar in an effort to map the wreck with stereo photos. The site's steep slope compelled the archaeologists to resort to a basic mapping technique that uses measuring tapes and plumb bobs to record the position of each of the artifacts.*

*A four-handled copper ingot weighing about 60 pounds—or one talent, as traders in the 14th century BC would have put it—starts its cautious ascent to the surface on a tray lifted by an air-filled balloon.*

# SUNKEN CARGO OF RAW RICHES

It was evident from the earliest dives on the wreck that the loss of the vessel at Ulu Burun must have dealt a staggering financial blow to the shippers who packed her hold. The cargo consisted principally of valuable raw materials, chief among them copper and tin, the ingredients of the substance that gave the Bronze Age its name.

Alloyed with tin, the more than 10 tons of copper aboard could have outfitted an army of 500 with bronze helmets and corselets and equipped it with 5,000 bronze spearheads and 5,000 bronze swords. Stacked alongside the copper was close to a ton of tin.

Both metals were shipped as ingots, most cast in the four-handled shape believed to have been contrived as the best form in which to load the raw metal onto pack animals. It is likely that donkey caravans brought the copper to port from Cypriot smelting works and the tin to the Syrian coast from perhaps as far away as Afghanistan.

The other materials aboard—ebony-like blackwood from tropical Africa, amber from northern Europe, and the ivory, resin, and glass pictured here—had equally remote origins. On reaching their destinations, most would have soon been converted to tools, weapons, and ornaments.

*A diver carefully chisels concrete-hard marine encrustation from a row of copper ingots. Apparently to prevent slippage on the rolling ship, the slabs were stacked like shingles on the side of a house, in overlapping layers. A pair of tin ingots— one bun shaped, the other a quarter of a four-handled ingot (inset, right)—are pitted and blistered from corrosion.*

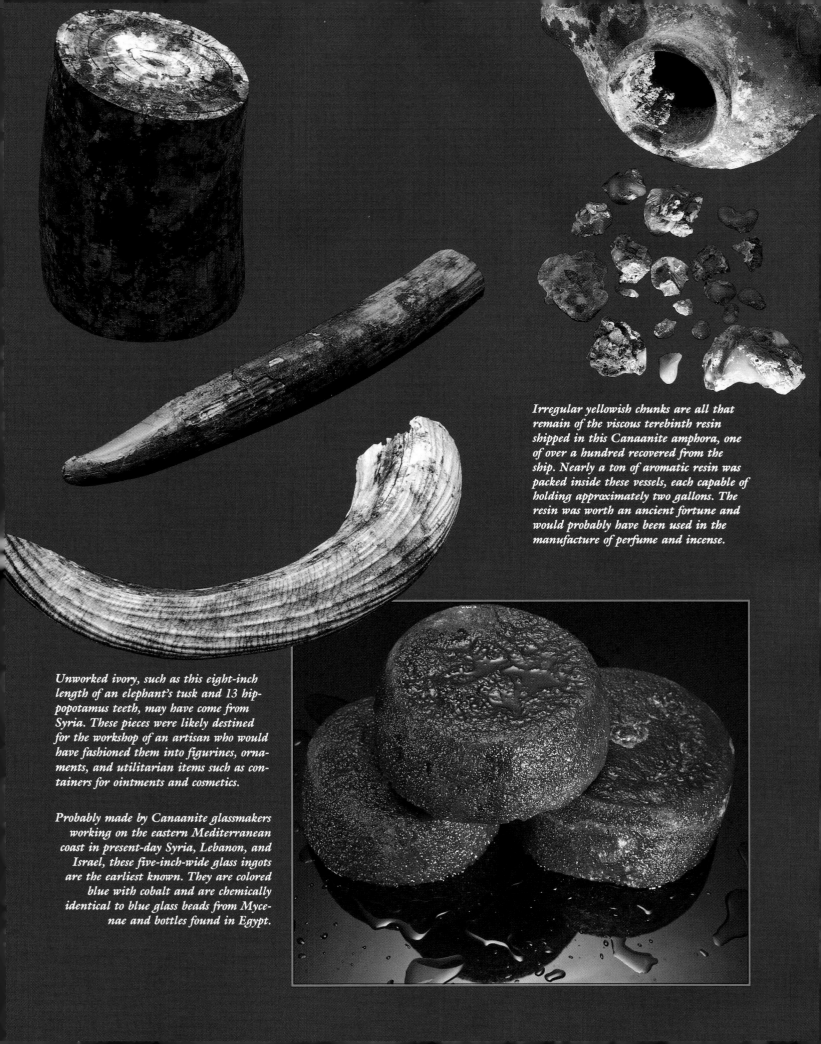

Irregular yellowish chunks are all that remain of the viscous terebinth resin shipped in this Canaanite amphora, one of over a hundred recovered from the ship. Nearly a ton of aromatic resin was packed inside these vessels, each capable of holding approximately two gallons. The resin was worth an ancient fortune and would probably have been used in the manufacture of perfume and incense.

Unworked ivory, such as this eight-inch length of an elephant's tusk and 13 hippopotamus teeth, may have come from Syria. These pieces were likely destined for the workshop of an artisan who would have fashioned them into figurines, ornaments, and utilitarian items such as containers for ointments and cosmetics.

Probably made by Canaanite glassmakers working on the eastern Mediterranean coast in present-day Syria, Lebanon, and Israel, these five-inch-wide glass ingots are the earliest known. They are colored blue with cobalt and are chemically identical to blue glass beads from Mycenae and bottles found in Egypt.

# IMPLEMENTS OF A COSMOPOLITAN SOCIETY

Among the first bronze artifacts recovered from the wreck was a heavily encrusted 13-inch-long dagger. It proved to be of Canaanite origin and was cast sometime during the second millennium BC on the Syro-Palestinian coast. Such items often provide marine archaeologists with the clues they need to pinpoint a ship's nationality. But in the case of the Ulu Burun wreck, the ancient dagger was only one of many inconclusive pieces in the persistent puzzle of her origin.

Also recovered from the wreck were arms and tools whose design marked them as Cypriot, Mycenaean, Canaanite, and Egyptian. They may have been commodities en route to market, the personal possessions of passengers and crewmen, or the contents of the ship's armory and carpenter's toolbox.

However, their presence aboard the ship vastly enriches knowledge of Bronze Age trade. Scholars believe that merchantmen of the era sailed the Mediterranean in a circular, counterclockwise pattern that took them from Syria-Palestine to Cyprus, into the Aegean, sometimes as far west as Sardinia, and back to North Africa and Egypt. The diverse origins of the ship's bronze implements and its cargo hint of a cosmopolitan trade network extending well beyond those busy ports deep into Europe, central Asia, and Africa. The bronze weapons aboard may have helped protect this ship from pirates preying on the sea lanes. And the bronze tools are probably similar to those used to build the vessels that made this international trade possible.

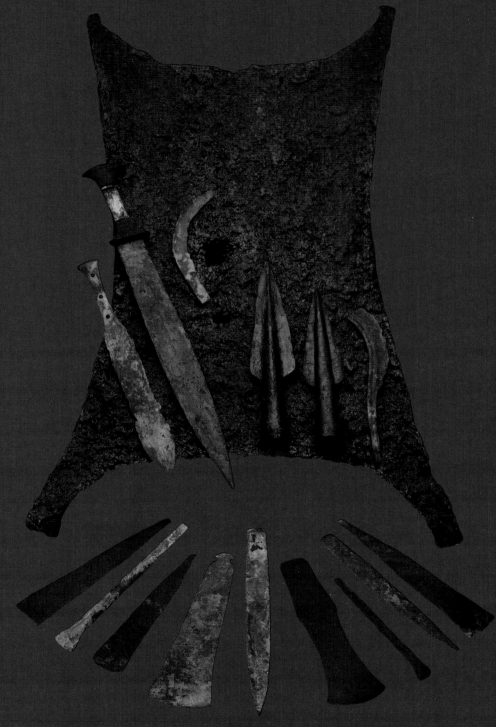

*Arrayed on top of a four-handled copper ingot are, from left to right, a bronze dagger, sword (also pictured inset opposite), and sickle, two bronze spearheads, and a bronze razor. Below them lies a collection of bronze ax and adz blades, chisels, and a drill bit.*

*At right, archaeologist Faith Hentschel lifts an 18-inch-long Canaanite sword from the seabed. The sword (inset, top) was cast in one piece. Its handle is inlaid with African blackwood and ivory, and has been preserved by a thick mantle of marine encrustation. The ribbed blade and flanged grip of the sword (lower inset), found three feet away, mark it as Mycenaean. Rivets in the holes in the grip and blade once held its hilt plate.*

# GLISTENING GOLD AMID THE KITCHEN POTS

When the ship disintegrated, several giant clay jars called pithoi broke free from their lashings and tumbled out onto the seabed. Bass, who had seen such jars pictured on ships in an Egyptian painting, assumed they were for fresh water.

But when a pithos tilted while being raised, divers were surprised to see broken pottery rain from its mouth. They gently extracted 18 pottery items—bowls, lamps, and jugs—some nested in neat stacks as if packed in a china barrel by a mover. The pottery solved a puzzle about the vessel's movements. "This ship was definitely coming from Cyprus," Bass declared. He recognized the rustic, assymetrical look of Cypriot ware, shaped without potter's wheels.

Another big surprise came when a surfacing diver announced to his jubilant colleagues crowding the *Virazon*'s rail that he had found a gold chalice. To archaeology, gold is no more precious than clay. But it could indicate this was something other than a common trading voyage—perhaps a royal mission, a possibility strengthened by all the militarily useful metal aboard.

Still, a simple clay drinking cup, a kylix, proved a more important find than the chalice. The chalice defied efforts to discern its date or origin. But the kylix's Mycenaean style suggested that it was made in the Aegean, probably in the 14th century BC—giving the first clue to the date of the disaster.

*A diver removes a juglet from a storage jar that started spilling pottery when lifted by balloon, while George Bass steadies the jar. It was so encrusted with 33 centuries of marine growth and sediment that at first it was mistaken for a boulder.*

At the site of their discovery (below), excavation director Cemal Pulak holds a small flask and the kylix that is reproduced at left. The gold chalice seen in the lower left inset still lies half-buried here, next to a large amphora.

Elegant in its double-handled simplicity, its red decorative swirls softened by millennia beneath the sea, the terra-cotta kylix above rivals in beauty the gleaming gold chalice below. Strangely, the two cups—one for everyday use and the other probably ceremonial—were found close together beneath the sand. The chalice is fashioned of upper and lower cones held together by rivets concealed by a collar.

# PRECIOUS LINKS TO VANISHED WORLDS

Archaeologists had never worked so long on a shipwreck. In nine years they logged some 20,000 dives and almost 5,500 hours of underwater time. In the process they recovered 4,000 artifacts and an additional 10,000 other items ranging from seeds to potsherds, all in their own way opening small windows onto vanished cultures.

The gold falcon pendant opposite at top right, for instance, is thought to be a 14th-century BC product of Canaan. Below the pendant, a hematite cylinder seal and its impression in clay provide a brief lesson in history—and in recycling. On the clay, a king faces a goddess over the head of a small priest, carved by a Babylonian artisan in about 1750 BC. The seal was still in use four centuries later, when the warrior and griffinlike figure in the middle were added in the style of the Assyrians.

At bottom right is one of the dig's most valued prizes: a diptych, with ivory hinges and boxwood covers designed to hold wax that could be inscribed with a stylus. Until its discovery, the earliest such "book" dated from the late eighth-century BC. A similar thrill was occasioned by finding the gold scarab below, which bears in hieroglyphs the name of Egypt's glamorous Queen Nefertiti—the first object ever found in Asia Minor or the Aegean to name her or her husband, the heretical pharaoh Akhenaten.

*A scarab whose underside bears the name of Nefertiti (above)—the only gold scarab of the famous queen ever found—is little more than half an inch long. To avoid losing or damaging such tiny artifacts, the diver at left employs an airlift hose with great caution while brushing sediment from a horn-shaped gold pendant.*

The minute size of these items reveals the difficulties archaeologists faced in searching for buried artifacts. The wingspan of the gold falcon (right) is less than 2½ inches. The cylinder seal (middle picture) stands little more than an inch high. Each leaf of the diptych (bottom) is almost four inches high, but it was found in 25 tiny pieces in a pithos full of sand and pomegranate remnants.

# CIVILIZATIONS BORN FROM THE SEA

Greek mythology tells of a legendary king of Athens named Aegeus who threw himself into the sea when he was mistakenly led to believe that his son, Theseus, had been killed by the Minotaur on the island of Crete. Known thereafter as the Aegean, that sea, its islands, and its shores stretching from Greece to Turkey were home to several great Bronze Age civilizations that were themselves long thought to be the stuff of folklore and myth.

These Aegean cultures had their roots in the Neolithic period, from the sixth through the fourth millennium BC, when the advent of agriculture led to increased settlement in the area. The importance of obsidian, a volcanic glass that could be fashioned into sharp-bladed tools and weapons and that was found in quantity on the island of Melos, sparked the beginning of a trading network throughout the region. In their travels, Aegean traders likely came in contact with ideas emanating from the powerful and literate civilizations of Mesopotamia and Egypt. By 3000 BC, the people of these fertile river valleys had begun to establish city-states, develop metallurgy, build monumental architecture, and create clearly defined social classes. Although they were doubtless influenced by these achievements, the nascent Aegean societies would nevertheless take at least 1,000 years to attain similar levels.

Over the course of the 2,500-year span of the Bronze Age—which scholars divide into Early, Middle, and Late periods—a handful of distinct but related cultures emerged in the separate geographical areas of the Aegean: the Cycladic in the islands of the Cyclades, the Trojan in western Anatolia, the Minoan on Crete, and the Helladic on mainland Greece. Progressing at different rates, each had its own moment in the sun and, at its height, influenced the others. Archaeologists generally associate the Early Bronze Age with the Cycladic and Trojan civilizations, the Middle with the Minoans, and the Late with the Helladic group known as the Mycenaeans.

## EARLY BRONZE AGE
## 3500-2000 BC

**CYCLADIC HEAD**

At the beginning of the Bronze Age, the southern limits of the Aegean realm—Crete and the islands of the Cyclades—were superbly positioned to take in the heady changes going on in such places as Egypt, which was entering its dynastic period and already exhibiting enormous sophistication and maturity. Expanding the system of commerce that had begun with the obsidian trade in the Neolithic period, seafaring islanders served as a conduit for new concepts, helping to spread them to other Aegean societies on their trading routes.

Despite this diffusion of ideas, the Aegean's various indigenous groups developed along relatively independent lines, as is readily apparent to archaeologists. The fortified walls of early Troy, for example, along with the hoard of treasure behind them, suggests the evolution of a strong political organization. In contrast, advances in art and technology were apparently central to the development of the Cyclades. Metallurgy, the cornerstone of Aegean civilization, flourished there, and the sculpted marble heads produced by Cycladic artists, stunning in their simplicity *(above)*, represent the highest aesthetic form of the time in the Aegean world.

The arrival of Indo-Europeans after 2000 BC foreshadowed a new age in the region. The destruction of old settlements and the appearance of new styles of pottery, architecture, and burial practices—as well as a new language, a precursor of Greek—indicate significant upheaval. Excavations reveal that the mainland and nearby island civilizations suffered a period of almost universal decline from which they would not recover until Mycenaean times.

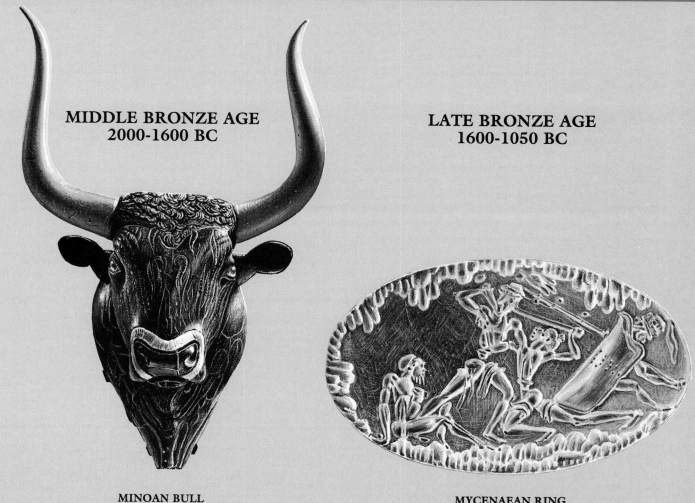

## MIDDLE BRONZE AGE
## 2000-1600 BC

## LATE BRONZE AGE
## 1600-1050 BC

**MINOAN BULL**

**MYCENAEAN RING**

Untouched by disturbances elsewhere, Minoan civilization on Crete blossomed. Named for a legendary king or series of kings called Minos, this culture was the first in the Aegean to contribute lasting achievements comparable to those of other major civilizations in the ancient world.

Palaces, first constructed on Crete around 1900 BC, were the center of Minoan life. The complexity of the buildings bespeaks a rich urban culture complete with social hierarchy, administrative bureaucracy, religious ritual, and organized craft production. Repeatedly damaged by earthquakes and fire, the palaces were totally rebuilt around 1700 BC, spurring a renaissance that is known as the Golden Age of Minoan civilization.

Peace, prosperity, and social equilibrium enabled the citizens of Crete to dominate the eastern Mediterranean, exerting an influence felt for many centuries. Their contributions included innovations in engineering, metallurgy, and governance. The Minoans also developed systems of writing that were almost entirely original. The first was a pictographic or hieroglyphic form written on clay, which was succeeded by the still-undeciphered script called Linear A.

Perhaps the most enduring legacy of the Minoans is their art. Cretan artists painted, carved, and sculpted ageless masterpieces of grace and beauty, depicting the natural world, religious themes, and sacred symbols such as the bull *(above)*. All over the Aegean and eastern Mediterranean, Minoan art was admired and imitated, most notably in the town of Akrotiri on the nearby island of Thera. Ironically, the destruction wrought by a massive volcanic eruption on Thera sometime around 1600 BC may have been what precipitated the demise of Minoan preeminence.

The cataclysmic Theran eruption was followed by the wholesale ruination of Cretan palaces—except at Knossos—by a combination of invasion and other natural disasters such as earthquakes. At the same time, a fusion of Minoan and Helladic culture on the mainland culminated in the birth of a new political entity, named for its most important citadel, Mycenae.

The Mycenaean civilization was distinctly militaristic. Towns were heavily fortified, and art often featured battle scenes and hunting forays. Wresting power from the Minoans, the mainlanders took over the palace at Knossos, as well as trade routes and even the Cretan writing system. Linear B, as the Mycenaean script is called, was a version of the Minoan system adapted to Greek.

Ambitious and powerful kings amassed a profusion of gold and silver treasures, such as the ring above, which were interred with them after death. Some of their earliest tombs, the shaft graves in Mycenae, were simply more elaborate versions of Middle Helladic burials set apart by special enclosures. Later in the period, however, domed burial chambers called tholoi were constructed and are magnificent examples of Mycenaean architecture and engineering.

During the Late Bronze Age, the Mycenaeans had attained hegemony in the Aegean, but their civilization, like that of the Minoans before them, eventually began to crumble. Although scholars dispute the causes—citing internal revolt, invasion, and environmental upheaval as possible explanations—they agree that the outcome was nothing less than total collapse. The ancient realms of the Aegean were all but forgotten for 300 years until they reemerged in the epic tales of Homer.

# ACKNOWLEDGMENTS

*The editors wish to thank the following for their valuable assistance in the preparation of this volume:*

Manfred Bietak, Austrian Archaeological Institute, Cairo; Horst Blanck, Istituto Archeologico Germanico, Rome; Wilfried Bölke, Heinrich Schliemann Museum, Ankershagen; Mike Braunlin, University of Cincinnati, Cincinnati, Ohio; Ann Brown, Ashmolean Museum, Oxford; Alice M. Cornell, University of Cincinnati, Cincinnati, Ohio; Christos Doumas, Athens; Klaus-Valtin von Eicksted, Deutsches Archäologisches Institut, Athens; Irmgard Ernstmeier, Munich; Klaus Goldman, Ingrid Griesa, Museum für Vor- und Frühgeschichte SMPK, Berlin; Maria Jacobsen, Institute of Nautical Archaeology, College Station, Texas; David Jordan, American School of Classical Studies at Athens; Klaus Junker, Deutsches Archäologisches Institut, Berlin; Heidi Klein, Bildarchiv Preussischer Kulturbesitz, Berlin; Manfred Korfmann, Hanswulf Bloedhorn, Institut für Vor- und Frühgeschichte, Tübingen; George Korres, Athens; Nanno Marinatos, Athens; Edith Meissner, Public Relations, Daimler-Benz, Stuttgart; Andromache Melas, Athens; Ellen Morate, National Archaeological Museum, Athens; Georgia Moschovakou, Ekdotike Athenon S.A., Athens; Cemal Pulak, Institute of Nautical Archaeology, College Station, Texas; Michael Sage, University of Cincinnati, Cincinnati, Ohio; Jannis Sakellarakis, Athens; Catherine Sease, Field Museum of Natural History, Chicago; Michael Siebler, Frankfurt; Emily Vermeule, Department of the Classics, Harvard University, Cambridge, Massachusetts.

# PICTURE CREDITS

New York/Museum of Cycladic Art, Athens (2); John Bigelow Taylor, New York/National Museum, Athens; John Bigelow Taylor, New York/Museum of Cycladic Art, Athens (2). 62, 63: Ekdotike Athenon S.A., Athens; Christos Doumas, Athens. 64, 65: John Bigelow Taylor, New York/Ashmolean Museum, Oxford—John Bigelow Taylor, New York; map by Time-Life Books. 66: Christos Doumas, Athens—Hirmer Fotoarchiv, Munich. 67: Ekdotike Athenon S.A., Athens. 68, 69: Hirmer Fotoarchiv, Munich. 71: Nimatallah/Art Resource, New York. 72, 73: Nimatallah/Art Resource, New York; Nanno Marinatos, Athens. 74, 75: Nimatallah/Ricciarini, Milan. 76: Ekdotike Athenon S.A., Athens. 77: Nimatallah/Ricciarini, Milan; Hirmer Fotoarchiv, Munich. 78, 79: Nimatallah/Ricciarini, Milan. 80: C. M. Dixon, Canterbury, Kent. 82-84: Otis Imboden, © 1981 National Geographic Society. 85: J. A. Sakellarakis, courtesy of the National Geographic Society. 86: Scala, Florence; Ekdotike Athenon S.A., Athens. 88, 89: P. Warren, Bristol, England. 91: Ekdotike Athenon S.A., Athens—from *The Palace of Minos at Knossos* by Sir Arthur Evans, Vol. 3, Macmillan, London, 1930. 92: Michael Holford/British Museum, London—Ashmolean Museum, Oxford. 93: Scala, Florence. 94: C. M. Dixon, Canterbury, Kent. 95: Professor J. A. MacGillivray and H. L. Sackett/British School at Athens. 96: Cliché, École Française d'Archéologie, Athens. 97: Ekdotike Athenon S.A., Athens. 99: Ekdotike Athenon S.A., Athens—Otis Imboden, © 1981 National Geographic Society—Ekdotike Athenon S.A., Athens (2); copyright British Museum, London. 100-103: Ekdotike Athenon S.A., Athens. 105: C. M.

Dixon, Canterbury, Kent. 107: © Erich Lessing, Vienna, Austria. 108, 109: Artephot/Nimatallah—Gordon W. Gahan, © 1978 National Geographic Society—Bildarchiv Preussischer Kulturbesitz, Berlin/Herakleion, Archäologisches Museum; Gianni Dagli Orti, Paris. 110, 111: Background D. & I. Mathioulakis, Athens, from *Crete—Archeological and Historical Sites, Scenery, Traditional Costumes.* Insets Ekdotike Athenon S.A., Athens (2); C. M. Dixon, Canterbury, Kent; Nimatallah/Art Resource, New York. 112, 113: Luisa Ricciarini, Milan; Leonard von Matt; Ekdotike Athenon S.A., Athens. 114: F. H. C. Birch/Sonia Halliday Photographs, Weston Turville, Buckinghamshire—Ekdotike Athenon S.A., Athens; Gianni Dagli Orti, Paris. 115: Gordon W. Gahan, © 1978 National Geographic Society. 116: C. M. Dixon, Canterbury, Kent—Robert Frerck/Woodfin Camp & Associates, New York. 117: Gianni Dagli Orti, Paris—F. H. C. Birch/Sonia Halliday Photographs, Weston Turville, Buckinghamshire. 118: Nikos Kontos, Athens—Ekdotike Athenon S.A., Athens. 120, 121: Hirmer Fotoarchiv, Munich. 122, 123: Ekdotike Athenon S.A., Athens (2)—bottom, University of Cincinnati, photo by Alison Frantz. 127: Base art by Time-Life Books. From *History of the Hellenic World: Prehistory and Protohistory*, Ekdotike Athenon S.A., Athens; Nikos Kontos, Athens; Artephot/Nimatallah. 128, 129: Base art by Time-Life Books; Gianni Dagli Orti, Paris; Scala, Florence; Ekdotike Athenon S.A., Athens; National Archaeological Museum, Athens; Artephot/Nimatallah; Ekdotike Athenon S.A., Athens. 130, 131: Princeton University Press and University of Cincinnati, watercolor by Piet de Jong. Carl Blegen and Marion

Rawson, *The Palace of Nestor at Pylos,* Vol. 1, Pt. 1, 1966, frontispiece—Princeton University Press and University of Cincinnati, photo by Alison Frantz. Carl Blegen and Marion Rawson, *The Palace of Nestor at Pylos,* Vol. 1, Pt. 2, 1966, plate 10. 133: Ekdotike Athenon S.A., Athens. 134, 135: Nikos Kontos, Athens—Mike Andrews/Susan Griggs Agency, London. 136, 137: Gianni Dagli Orti, Paris, except bottom left, Ekdotike Athenon S.A., Athens. 138: Hirmer Fotoarchiv, Munich; Ekdotike Athenon S.A., Athens—Hirmer Fotoarchiv, Munich. 139: Luisa Ricciarini, Milan—Lotos Film, Eberhard Thiem, Kaufbeuren/National Museum, Athens; Robert Harding Picture Library, London. 140: Ekdotike Athenon S.A., Athens. 141: National Archaeological Museum, Athens. 143: Map by Time-Life Books based on a map in *History of the Hellenic World: Prehistory and Protohistory* published by Ekdotike Athenon S.A., Athens. 144: Nikos Kontos, Athens. 145: Nikos Kontos, Athens; Ekdotike Athenon S.A., Athens. 147: © Bill Curtsinger. 148: © Bill Curtsinger—Donald A. Frey/Institute of Nautical Archaeology. 149: Donald A. Frey/Institute of Nautical Archaeology. 150: Donald A. Frey/Institute of Nautical Archaeology—© Bill Curtsinger (2). 151, 152: © Bill Curtsinger. 153: Donald A. Frey/Institute of Nautical Archaeology, courtesy National Geographic Society—Donald A. Frey/Institute of Nautical Archaeology. 154: © Bill Curtsinger. 155: © Bill Curtsinger (2); Donald A. Frey/Institute of Nautical Archaeology. 156: Donald A. Frey/Institute of Nautical Archaeology; © Bill Curtsinger. 157: © Bill Curtsinger (2)—Donald A. Frey/Institute of Nautical Archaeology. 158, 159: Art by Paul Breeden.

# BIBLIOGRAPHY

## BOOKS

Andronicos, Manolis. *National Museum*. Athens: Ekdotike Athenon S.A., 1990.

Blegen, Carl W. *Troy and the Trojans* (Ancient Peoples and Places series). New York: Frederick A. Praeger, 1963.

Blegen, Carl W., and Marion Rawson. *The Palace of Nestor at Pylos in Western Messenia* (Vol. 1). Princeton, N.J.: Princeton University Press, 1966.

Boardman, John. *Greek Art* (rev. ed.). London: Thames and Hudson, 1985.

Burkert, Walter. *Greek Religion*. Translated by John Raffan. Cambridge, Mass.: Harvard University Press, 1985.

Castleden, Rodney. *The Knossos Labyrinth*. London: Routledge, 1990.

Chadwick, John:
*The Decipherment of Linear B* (2d ed.). Cambridge: Cambridge University Press, 1967.
*Linear B and Related Scripts*. London: British Museum Publications, 1989.
*The Mycenaean World*. Cambridge: Cambridge University Press, 1976.

Cottrell, Leonard. *The Bull of Minos: The Discoveries of Schliemann and Evans*. New York: Facts On File Publications, 1984.

Demargne, Pierre. *The Birth of Greek Art*. Translated by Stuart Gilbert and James Emmons. New York: Golden Press, 1964.

Dickinson, O. T. P. K. *The Origins of Mycenaean Civilisation*. Göteborg: Paul Aströms Förlag, 1977.

Doumas, Christos:
*Santorini: A Guide to the Island and Its Archaeological Treasures*. Athens: Ekdotike Athenon S.A., 1989.
*Santorini: The Prehistoric City of Akroteri*. Athens: Editions Hannibal, n.d.
*Thera: Pompeii of the Ancient Aegean*. London: Thames and Hudson, 1983.

Eisler, Riane. *The Chalice and the Blade: Our History, Our Future*. San Francisco: Harper & Row, 1987.

Evans, Arthur. *The Palace of Minos at Knossos* (3 vols.). London: Macmillan, 1921-1930.

Fitton, J. Lesley. *Cycladic Art*. London: British Museum Publications, 1989.

Graham, J. Walter. *The Palaces of Crete* (rev. ed.). Princeton, N.J.: Princeton University Press, 1987.

Hampe, Roland, and Erika Simon. *Un Millénaire d'Art Grec 1600-600*. Fribourg: Office du Livre, 1980.

Hardy, D. A., et al. (Eds.). *Thera and the Aegean World III* (Vol. 1). London: Thera Foundation, 1990.

Higgins, Reynold. *Minoan and Mycenaean Art* (rev. ed.). London: Thames and Hudson, 1985.

Hood, Sinclair:
*The Arts in Prehistoric Greece*. Harmondsworth, Middlesex, U.K.: Penguin Books, 1978.
*The Minoans: The Story of Bronze Age Crete*. New York: Praeger Publishers, 1971.

Immerwahr, Sara A. *Aegean Painting in the Bronze Age*. University Park, Penna.: Pennsylvania State University Press, 1990.

Karageorghis, Vassos. *The Cyprus Museum*. Translated by A. H. Kromholz and S. Foster Kromholz. Nicosia, Cyprus: C. Epiphaniou Publications, 1989.

Kean, Victor J. *The Disk from Phaistos*. Athens: Efstathiadis Group, 1985.

Kofou, Anna. *Crete: All the Museums and Archeological Sites*. Athens: Ekdotike Athenon S.A., 1990.

Korfmann, Manfred. "Troy: Topography and Navigation." In *Troy and the Trojan War*, edited by Machteld J. Mellink. Bryn Mawr, Penna.: Bryn Mawr College, 1986.

Luce, J. V. *The End of Atlantis*. London: Thames and Hudson, 1969.

McDonald, William A., and Carol G. Thomas. *Progress into the Past* (2d ed.). Bloomington: Indiana University Press, 1990.

Marangou, Lila (Ed.). *Cycladic Culture: Naxos in the 3rd Millennium BC*. Translated by Alex Doumas. Athens: Nicholas P. Goulandris Foundation—Museum of Cycladic Art, 1990.

Marinatos, Nannó. *Art and Religion in Thera*. Athens: D. & I. Mathioulakis, n.d.

Marinatos, Spyridon. *Crete and Mycenae*. New York: Harry N. Abrams, n.d.

Michailidou, Anna. *Knossos: A Complete Guide to the Palace of Minos*. Athens: Ekdotike Athenon S.A., 1991.

Morgan, Lyvia. *The Miniature Wall Paintings of Thera*. Cambridge: Cambridge University Press, 1988.

Mylonas, George E. *Mycenae: Rich in Gold*. Athens: Ekdotike Athenon S.A., 1983.

Page, Denys L. *History and the Homeric Iliad*. Berkeley: University of California Press, 1959.

Pinsent, John. *Greek Mythology* (rev. ed.). Twickenham, Middlesex, U.K.: Newnes Books, 1986.

Platon, Nicholas. *Zakros: The Discovery of a Lost Palace of Ancient Crete*. London: Thames and Hudson, 1969.

Poole, Lynn, and Gray Poole. *One Passion, Two Loves*. New York: Thomas Y. Crowell, 1966.

*Prehistory and Protohistory* (History of the Hellenic World). University Park, Penna.: Pennsylvania State University Press, 1974.

Renfrew, Colin. *The Cycladic Spirit*. London: Thames and Hudson, 1991.

Renfrew, Colin, and Malcolm Wagstaff (Eds.). *An Island Polity: The Archaeology of Exploitation in Melos*. Cambridge: Cambridge University Press, 1982.

Sakellarakis, J. A., and E. Sapouna-Sakellaraki. *Archanes*. Athens: Ekdotike Athenon S.A., 1991.

Schliemann, Heinrich. *Troy and Its Remains*. Bronx, N.Y.: Benjamin Blom, 1968 (reprint of 1875 edition).

Siebler, Michael. *Troia-Homer-Schliemann: Mythos und Wahrheit*. Mainz am Rhein: Philipp von Zabern, 1990.

Simpson, R. Hope, and O. T. P. K. Dickinson. *A Gazetteer of Aegean Civilisation in the Bronze Age, Vol. I: The Mainland and Islands* (Studies in Mediterranean Archaeology, Vol. 52). Göteborg: Paul Aströms Förlag, 1979.

Sperling, Jerome. "Reminiscences of Troy." In *Troy and the Trojan War*, edited by Machteld J. Mellink. Bryn Mawr, Penna.: Bryn Mawr College, 1986.

Taylour, Lord William. *The Mycenaeans* (rev. ed.) (Ancient Peoples and

Places series). London: Thames and Hudson, 1983.

Thucydides. *History of the Peloponnesian War, Books I and II*. Translated by Charles Forster Smith. Cambridge, Mass.: Harvard University Press, 1980.

Vermeule, Emily. *Greece in the Bronze Age*. Chicago: University of Chicago Press, 1972.

Warren, Peter. *The Aegean Civilizations*. New York: Peter Bedrick Books, 1989.

Wood, Michael. *In Search of the Trojan War*. New York: Facts On File Publications, 1985.

Wright, James C. *Thanatos: Les Coutumes Funéraires en Égée à l'Age du Bronze*. Edited by Robert Laffineur. Liège: Université de l'État à Liège, 1987.

## PERIODICALS

Bass, George F. "Oldest Known Shipwreck Reveals Bronze Age Splendors." *National Geographic*, December 1987.

Bass, George F., et al. "The Bronze Age Shipwreck at Ulu Burun: 1986 Campaign." *American Journal of Archaeology*, 1989, Vol. 93.

Betancourt, Philip P. "The End of the Greek Bronze Age." *Antiquity*, March 1976.

Doumas, Christos G. "High Art from the Time of Abraham." *Biblical Archaeology Review*, January/February 1991.

Fleischman, John. "Digging Deeper into the Mysteries of Troy." *Smithsonian*, January 1992.

Judge, Joseph. "Greece's Brilliant Bronze Age." *National Geographic*, February 1978.

Kilian, Klaus. "The Emergence of *Wanax* Ideology in the Mycenaean Palaces." *Oxford Journal of Archaeology*, November 1988.

Marinatos, Spyridon. "Thera: Key to the Riddle of Minos." *National Geographic*, May 1972.

Ottaway, James H., Jr. "New Assault on Troy." *Archaeology*, September/October 1991.

Pulak, Cemal. "The Bronze Age Shipwreck at Ulu Burun, Turkey: 1985 Campaign." *American Journal of Archaeology*, 1988, Vol. 92.

Sakellarakis, Jannis, and Efi Sapouna-Sakellaraki. "Drama of Death in a Minoan Temple." *National Geographic*, February 1981.

Shaw, Ian. "Statue Sheds New Light on 'Life of Zeus'." *Daily Telegraph*, September 21, 1990.

Warren, Peter. "Knossos: New Excavations and Discoveries." *Archaeology*, July/August 1984.

## OTHER SOURCES

"Der Troianische Krieg . . . und Kein Ende." Videotape. Frankfurt: Lothar Spree Film Production, 1991.

Doumas, Christos. "Cycladic Art." Catalog. Washington, D.C.: National Gallery of Art, 1979.

Hägg, Robin, and Nanno Marinatos (Eds.). "The Minoan Thalassocracy: Myth and Reality." Proceedings of the Third International Symposium at the Swedish Institute in Athens, May 31-June 5, 1982.

Sakellarakis, J. A. "Herakleion Museum." Illustrated guide. Athens: Ekdotike Athenon S.A., 1991.

"Troy, Mycenae, Tiryns, Orchomenos: Heinrich Schliemann: The 100th Anniversary of his death." Catalog. Athens: Ministry of Culture—Greek Committee IOM—Museum für Ur- und Frühgeschichte der Staatlichen Museen zu Berlin, 1990.

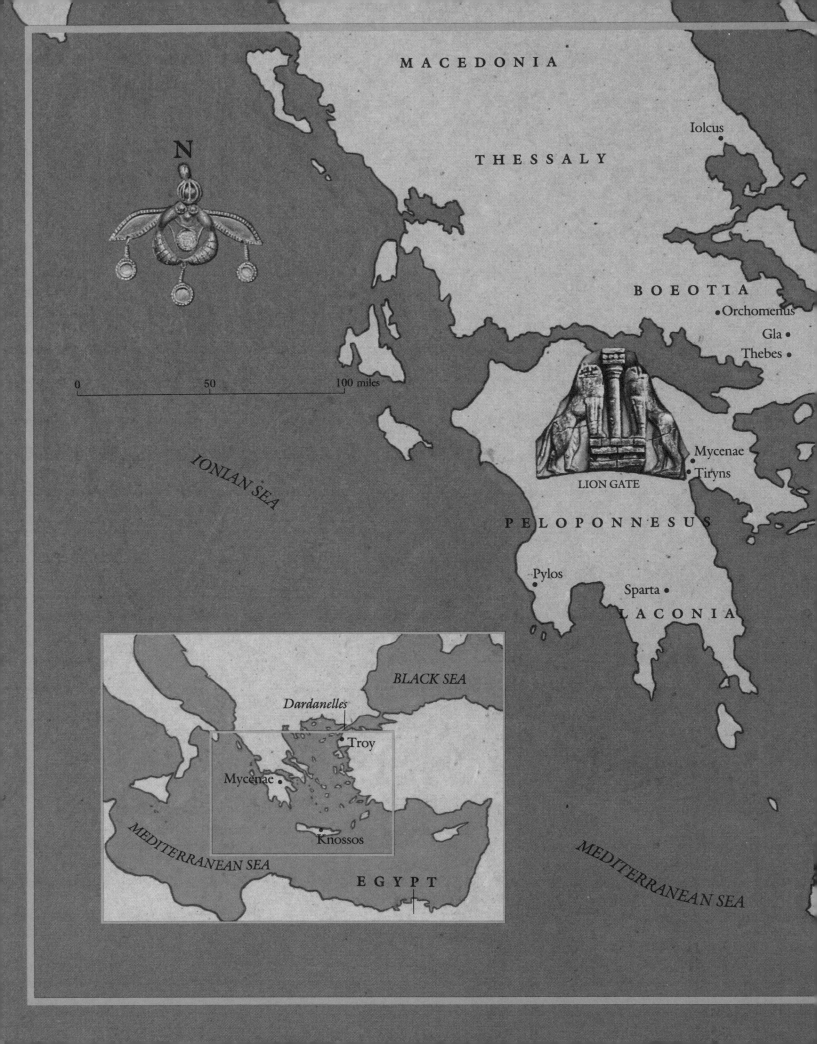

MACEDONIA

THESSALY

Iolcus

BOEOTIA

•Orchomenus

Gla •

Thebes •

N

IONIAN SEA

0        50        100 miles

LION GATE

Mycenae

Tiryns

PELOPONNESUS

Pylos

Sparta •

LACONIA

BLACK SEA

Dardanelles

Troy

Mycenae

MEDITERRANEAN SEA

Knossos

EGYPT

MEDITERRANEAN SEA